A RUNNING START

A RUNNING START

An Athlete, A Woman

by LYNDA HUEY

Quadrangle / The New York Times Book Co.

This book was prepared with the help of the Institute for the Study of Sport and Society.

Design by Tere LoPrete

Library of Congress Cataloging in Publication Data
Huey, Lynda.
    A running start.

    Autobiography.
    1. Huey, Lynda. 2. Track-athletics for
women. I. Title.
GV697.H83A37   1975   796.4'2'0924 [B]   74-24289
ISBN 0-8129-0523-7

Acknowledgments

I would like to thank a few people without whom this book would not have been possible:

NEIL, for starting the idea, even though the idea and I had to grow before it could become a book.

JONATHAN, who believed in this book and allowed it to be.

T.S., whose patience at a critical time allowed me to step out of my narrow little world.

B.G., who helped me free my mind, who always believed in me, and who makes life happier for me just because I know he's there.

GATESY, who cleaned up so many of my messes and gave so much of herself.

TRACY, my favorite audience.

P.J., my twin sister—finally!

MICKI, for never judging me, but helping me to see myself.

DANNY, for making me be real, even when I didn't want to be.

MARGIE, for her constant good, kind support.

BILL Who?, because he wouldn't let me keep playing that game.

ALAN, for his consistent good humor and insight.

TOMMIE LEE, for never letting me be mentally lazy.

UNCLE WILTIE, always a positive force and big brother influence.

LISA, who stepped in nobly to help complete this book.

BILLEE AND HERM, my East Coast mom and dad.

ALL THE PEOPLE who let me stay with them during my boll weevil days.

MY MOM AND DAD, who have loved me deeply through it all —and only they know how much all is.

Contents

PREFACE   *ix*

INTRODUCTION   *3*

1. *A View from the Track* — *9*
2. *We've Got the Spirit* — *19*
3. *Pom-poms, Footballs, and Spikes* — *29*
4. *A Course in Frustration* — *41*
5. *Discovering that "Natural High"* — *51*
6. *A Patch of Blue, Huey Style* — *63*
7. *Separate and Unequal* — *73*
8. *The Speed City Era* — *85*
9. *Seventeen Units of Life* — *97*
10. *Black Changes, White Reactions* — *103*
11. *The Olympic Boycott Movement* — *111*
12. *Meanwhile, Where Were the Women?* — *123*
13. *Imitation Athletes* — *137*
14. *From the Ghetto to Cowtown* — *143*
15. *The Oberlin Experience* — *163*
16. *Looking at Sport Through Oberlin Eyes* — *179*
17. *Happy, Healthy, and Horny* — *197*
18. *A New Generation* — *213*
19. *An Athlete, A Woman* — *229*

Preface

"Some magazine would pay a fortune for my seventeen years' worth of diaries," I said, rubbing my hands together and making demonlike faces. I was talking with some of the competitors as the action unfolded at the men's National Amateur Athletic Union Track and Field Championships in Bakersfield, California.

Neil Amdur, a sportswriter for *The New York Times*, noticed this scene and overheard my comment about the diaries. Later that evening he approached me in the meet headquarters hotel and asked, "Do you really have seventeen years of diaries?"

"Yep, seventeen big ones," I answered.

"Now, I don't know what you've done the rest of your life, but I saw you in action tonight, and I can't help but wonder if you might be interested in doing a book."

That's where it all started. The book that Neil and I envisioned was to focus on the male superstars I've known over the years. (For various reasons, we never carried the project through.) The book I have written is quite a different thing. But at that time, I pretty much defined my life in terms of the men with whom I was involved.

The fact that I had a life of my own or that I had attempted to have an athletic career was of minor significance. But as the idea for this book grew and began to take shape, so did my feelings about my own importance. I realized that I had been a part of some interesting periods in sport, and that I had some insightful things to say, not only about male athletes, but also about the problems women face in their attempt to be serious athletes.

I had never given much thought to the discrimination that women face in sport. I was too busy basking in the reflected glory of my male superstars to realize that by so doing I was making up for my feelings of insignificance. I had dealt with big-time jocks on an equal basis in only one way, sex-as-sport, but I had been able to siphon off enough of their huge egos to keep mine full blown. But that was an artificial sense of importance that faded when a week or so went by with no superstar around. And the cycle repeated itself.

I was able to see this pattern in my life when, for the first time, I read my diaries and saw what I had to say about my life, each day, for seventeen years. I reflected on and analyzed my life and my sexual relationships. Although the fun portion of my life was the only part I had chosen to remember, I was now able to see that between those Super Bowls of laughs and chaos were moments of doubt and alienation. I was being driven by my desire to *prove* that I was special, not an emotional weakling of a woman.

From the first day that I started work on this book, I have been developing a different outlook on many things. The Institute for the Study of Sport and Society took over the project, and Micki and Jack Scott became my co-authors.

Now I was doing something meaningful, not just cheering on one of my male companions. In my diaries, starting with fourth grade and moving through my teenage years, I saw the trip I had been on. I realized that I had thrived on moments of cheerleader stardom, and from then on had wanted to be in the limelight. But the limelight was not easily available for me, so I had grabbed for it by associating with famous men. I had never stopped to think that the same recognition that the men were receiving should have been available to me as well. It wasn't, and I accepted that. I couldn't be taken seriously as someone who accomplishes, so I evolved into a clown who could keep 'em laughing.

The problem, of course, was that I never learned to take myself seriously. I knew I had intelligence, but I hardly exercised it, except to meet the challenge of out-talkin' and out-jivin' the guys. Even when I was teaching, my thoughts were on my work only when I was in the classroom; the rest of the time I was planning, scheming—always scheming—about the various men in my life. Even though I was a college professor, my responsibilities could be dropped at a moment's notice if a man with plans for fun came along. I had programmed myself to believe that my function was to entertain. Long ago I had *learned* that the ultimate goal of all women was to attract men, and I was making sure I stayed in the thick of the action. I would travel hundreds of miles to be in the social spotlight with the superstars. I thought that made me a star too. In some ways it did, but I hadn't yet established my own separate identity.

During the writing of this book, I lived in Carlsbad, California, overlooking the Pacific. I was living alone, and for the first time in my life I loved it. My discovery that even though no one else was in my house, I did not feel alone, was a major breakthrough. I had never experienced that before. I had been a "people freak" and always had company. Now the ocean, my typewriter, and my own thoughts and ambitions were my company. I had finally become my own best friend. I no longer had to stay on the move every minute to avoid those conversations with myself. As much as I loved the out-of-town visitors who stopped and spent time, I loved to see them go, too. I spent hours pouring my thoughts out on paper; I had outgrown my diary and was now keeping an overflowing journal.

While reading my diaries I discovered I could learn much from them. I could identify the problems and forces at work in each stage of my life; and once I identified the source of anxiety or doubts, it no longer had the same power over me. I began analyzing my current thoughts with the same eagerness. For the first time I was appraising myself honestly; it was a bit scary. My diary was the one companion that had never heard me lie. I found that my memories had distorted much. I had seen my life as one continuous series of fun and games, but the written words showed doubts, fears, and anxieties that I had never consciously admitted to myself, let alone to another listening ear.

People who knew me saw me as nearly invulnerable, always ready with a comeback. Gradually, however, I saw that for every strength, I had a weakness that I had previously been covering up with flippant word games and comedy routines. Now I was willing to uncover those camouflages and to dig into them. What motivated me? What was I really looking for as I ran at a fevered pace in and out of peoples' lives? Who was that masked woman?

I had always thought of my life as a comedy, but as I wrote this book I was seeing for the first time that it had tragic overtones. I saw that there were elements in this society that should and could be changed. Many of these thoughts were new to me. Within these last months my life has taken on new implications as I have been forced to sum up, to analyze, to criticize, and to suggest.

As I looked for pictures to illustrate the book, I became aware that although there were literally hundreds of pictures of me in my cheerleader uniform, not one photograph had recorded my high school athletic career. Although a few pictures had been taken of me during my college track and field hockey days, no one had kept or filed those pictures as had been done for the men athletes. My thoughts about the lack of recognition for women athletes began to gel.

Just when I thought I was finally getting my world together, the bottom fell out. Micki Scott had been staying at my beach apartment in Carlsbad working on the rough draft of this book. Jack Scott appeared on the scene one night and the next morning told me he and Micki had to leave immediately. I drove them to the airport, expecting to see them in Portland several weeks later. However, three days later, late at night, there was an unexpected banging on my door and a brisk shout of "Lynda Huey? FBI." Agents questioned me for a half hour and then dropped the bombshell: "While you were in the Scotts' apartment in New York, did you ever see anyone who looked like William and Emily Harris, or Patty Hearst?" Except for news reports this was the first time I had heard of Patty Hearst.

The next two weeks seemed surreal. I immediately left my apartment and drove to a friend's house. Two days later agents were questioning her. I visited one of my volleyball team members who had become a close friend—she was questioned the next day. I drove to Wilt Chamberlain's house in Bel Air, feeling protected in his fortress. I hadn't been there three hours before a caller on Wilt's unlisted telephone was asking if Micki was there. A week later, Wilt was phoned by the FBI. No matter where I went, or who I telephoned, the FBI was never far behind.

During this period I had several genuinely good experiences. Wilt, who had never seen me in moments of weakness, was surprised when I turned to him for support. Yet there he was, my big brother, offering me security and strength. Billy Gaines, a close friend in San Jose, hearing real fear in my voice over the telephone, flew to San Diego to be with me for the weekend. Alan Silber, my New York attorney and running buddy, told me, "Call me and have them pull me out of court if you need me. Don't worry, I'll be on call for you twenty-four hours a day." Patty Van Wolvelaere, my best female friend, kept her continual flow of positive energy turned in my direction. I knew I had a beautiful set of close friends.

I flew to New York to begin working with Lisa Wohl, a writer who my editor, Jonathan Segal, had supplied for me because of Micki's disappearance. The book took on a slightly different slant. Lisa's feminist viewpoint was injected into my material, and I wasn't sure how I felt about it. At first it caught me off guard to hear my own ideas sound so militant. I had never considered myself a griper, so I worried that the book sounded too resentful. But with the book finished now, I know that everything in it is definitely me, and that Lisa's contribution was a welcome addition.

Although I have said some harsh things that I think needed to be said, I also feel compelled to emphasize here the joy of living that has always been my main driving force. Athletics to me has been the root of the greatest satisfaction and happiness in my life. Basking in my successes, learning from my failures, pushing myself to the limits of my endurance, grinning at my crazy antics, and laughing at myself as I get carried away into scenes out of *North Dallas Forty*—*these* parts of the athletic experience will always remain the strongest in my memory.

Hopefully the unpleasant experiences I have had as a female in sport will continue to dwindle and will clear the way for the lucky women who choose to be the athletes of the future.

L.H., *New York*

A RUNNING START

Introduction

"Last call for the 100-yard dash!" sounds over the loud-speakers.

Eight of us finalists assemble at the starting line, ready to run. Sunny California has given us perfect track weather, about 75 degrees, clear, and no wind. The green tartan synthetic track is the best on the west coast. Its consistency and perfect resiliency should get some good performances out of us. In the three-ring circus that is the May 1968 San Jose State Women's Invitational Track and Field Meet, all eyes suddenly turn to us. The crowd waits expectantly, sizing us up. This is my home track and home crowd. I'm the only San Jose State sprinter to qualify for the finals of the 100-yard dash.

I know I'm going to run a good race. Just the right amount of adrenalin is roaring through my body. I warm up with a few fast high knee lifts to check my form. It's sharp and ready. A few practice starts assure me that I'm quick today. I bend over slowly, straight-legged, to test my hamstring muscles, the main gauge of my potential speed. On days that I feel no tension in the back of my upper thighs before a race, I know I'm in trouble. My hamstrings won't be ready to contract with the raw power I need. But if they're too tight, I face the possibility of straining or injuring those temperamental muscles. Today, my legs are talking to me and saying only good things. I feel a tension in them that will ease to a flexible looseness as I stretch them slowly.

I look around at the seven other women who nervously wait with me for the starting gun. At once I spot three who don't consider themselves contenders. With scattered glances and uneasy movement they look at the rest of us with real anxiety, and they don't seem to know what to do with their bodies in these last few moments before the race begins. Their concentration is already ruined; they're worried about us, not about what they have to do.

Chi Cheng, running for Pomona, is two places over from me in lane 5 and, as usual, looks beautiful. Trackwatchers are already calling her the most talented woman sprinter since Wilma Rudolph. With a slenderness that hides her strength, Chi is also credited with the prettiest form in women's track. Her long strides have a smoothness, a fluidity that makes her incredible speed seem almost effortless.

The woman in lane 4, next to me, is an unknown quantity. Tall, black, from Harbor Junior College, she looks as if she could be a tough sprinter. She already beat me in the semifinal, when I eased up trying to conserve energy for the final. I'm not sure whether she had been running full speed to my seven-eighths speed or if she too had been saving herself. Right now those lean, sinewy legs are telling three hundred people in the stands that she is a runner to watch. Ginger Smith from Stanford is in lane 6. I've bested her in three of the last four times we've competed in the 100, but blond, feisty Ginger is not a runner to count out.

We walk to the starting blocks, cocky sprinters, strutting, staring straight ahead. My every move projects assurance. I want the other runners to know I'm in control. I want them to be afraid of me. You can't beat someone you fear; we all know it, and we all play the same psychological game. The psychic energy flowing between lanes 3, 4, 5, and 6 is incredible. I rev up my energy level another notch to make myself the most aggressive.

We're shaking our thighs, swinging our arms, breathing deeply. Total body awareness. I concentrate on the physical explosion to come in the first few steps of the race.

"Runners come to your marks."

The psychological warfare escalates. No one wants to be first in the starting blocks. If you're ready early while your competitor is still positioning herself, you may have to wait another ten seconds—plenty of time to lose your concentration. I'm determined to be last. A couple of slow stretches, hands down on the track, then I extend my right leg and carefully place my foot on the block. Repeat with the left leg. Dust off each hand and place it perfectly on the starting line. Tighten the concentration. Focus eyes five yards down the track.

"Set!"

I'm set. Itchin' to explode out of the blocks. No confidence problems today. Shoot that gun, buddy!

The gun! My reaction to the gun is so fast it almost scares me. I'm out of the blocks even before Chi. Perfect start. My knees are pumping. My body is low in a powerful drive forward. My arms are controlling all that explosive force, channeling my energy directly toward the finish line.

We hit the 30-yard mark. Chi's tremendous acceleration is pulling her ahead. Ginger is outside my line of vision already—I've left her behind. I'm running side by side with the black woman from Harbor. She takes long strides; by comparison mine are quick, short, and pistonlike. We're even, each feeling the force of the other.

The 50-yard mark. I decide to try for more power. By moving my arms more vigorously I can accelerate the thrust in my legs. But careful! I have to judge precisely or I will upset the delicate balance of rhythm, powerful contraction, and relaxation that is speeding me forward. If I overestimate and try for too much power, I could "tie up" —have my muscles tighten, putting on the brakes rather than increasing my speed. But if I judge correctly, I can increase the power and the speed while still maintaining the proper amount of looseness in my stride.

My judgment is right. I feel a tremendous charge of power as my body responds smoothly to my will. I feel myself edge gradually away from the tall black girl. A moment of truth between us as she tries to match me. Then she lets me go and falls back outside my peripheral vision. Strength floods through my being. Visions of Wonder Woman flash through my head.

I can see Chi a yard or two ahead of me hitting the tape. I have to discipline myself to keep my sprint form and concentration all the way through the finish line. I lean low across the line to cheat those stopwatches ticking off the seconds.

Breathless, we walk around, waiting to hear the results. Blood throbs through my body. My eyes squint with the momentary fatigue that comes after all-out physical exertion. A moment of happiness and satisfaction is shared as Chi and I wrap an arm around each other. We had both run well. Then the announcer's voice booms out over the speaker. "In first place, with a time of 10.7, a new national collegiate record, Chi Cheng."

Wow! I knew we had been fast, but I didn't realize the race had been *that* fast.

"In second place, from San Jose State, Lynda Huey, with a time of 10.9."

I don't even hear the rest of the announcement. I can't

believe my ears. I ask all three timers to confirm the results. My lifetime best time! Only a month before my fastest time in the 100 was 11.4, but then each succeeding week I managed to bring my time down—11.3, 11.2, and—now. There is something frightening in my success, a challenge, a new responsibility to myself. I have proved my capacity to break through the 11-second barrier and can actually consider myself a national caliber sprinter. I can allow myself new goals that I couldn't even consider a month ago.

I let myself flow with the excitement and triumph of the moment. A lot of familiar faces are in the crowd, and a lot of those faces wear new looks of respect as I walk by. But I don't need their approval. I have just gained my own.

I didn't win the gold medal or set the record that day. In other meets I would win gold medals and even set a national collegiate record of my own. Yet at this moment I am completely satisfied. Chi has won the race, but I have won in the continuing race against myself. My body and mind have just totally expressed themselves. I have just run faster than I have ever run in my life. I know that on this day and in this race I have done my absolute best. I feel terrific!

1

→》》 《《←

A View from the Track

"You run in a track meet? You've got to be kidding." That was my greeting from the information director of San Jose State when I went to his office to talk about the upcoming San Jose Invitational. I was planning to run in the race I just described in the introduction; and, as a San Jose State junior, I'd been assigned by the organizers to try to get the meet some publicity help from the college. I got publicity all right, but for the wrong reasons.

"You don't look like a Russian shot-putter," the information director protested. "Can you really run?" He gave me a big wink. "Yeah, I bet you can. I bet you can really chase the guys and catch them."

At the time I took his comments as complimentary. I really could be *both* a girl and an athlete. In fact, this information director thought that cute little Lynda Huey, girl track star, was cute enough to rate an interview with Dan Hruby, sports columnist for the *San Jose Mercury*. The next day my picture appeared on the front page of the *Mercury*'s sports section. The accompanying article explained that I was doing my best "to erase the image of Tamara Press, the big burly Russian shot-putter, which still hangs over women's track and field."

Cute, pert, little, green-eyed, coy, attractive, 36-24-36—those were just some of the adjectives Hruby used to describe me. (I don't know where he got those measurements; I was in good shape but I'm an athlete, not a bathing beauty.) Still, a gimmick is a gimmick, and Hruby's article led to more publicity. I was invited to go be cute at a sportscaster's luncheon. There a local television reporter spotted me and asked me to go be cute on his interview show. Suddenly, my name and face were in the news. People around the San Jose State campus treated me with new respect. I received notes and phone calls from people I hadn't heard from in years.

I loved every second of this attention. At last, I was getting my share of the glory, the glory successful male athletes take for granted. At the time it didn't bother me that the press stories had stressed my looks, not the fact that I was just emerging as a national caliber sprinter. Only much later did I realize that the moral of each newspaper story was clear: a track athlete who qualified as a woman was so rare as to be newsworthy.

Marty Liquori, one of America's top male milers, recently hypothesized to me what I will call his theory on the "survival of the ugliest." According to Marty, "you can take two young girls of equal talent and ability, one being great looking and the other being ugly, and the great looking one won't stand a chance of making it in the athletic world. She'll have too many alternatives presented to her, too many social pressures put on her. But the ugly girl will probably stay with athletics as her one form of outlet for success and recognition."

What he seemed to be saying was an attractive woman athlete was a freak. I learned to think of myself as a rare exception to the typical sexless woman athlete. I learned to play cutesie, flirting games off the track to counteract any doubts about my "femininity." I didn't realize then that reconciling the female–athlete dichotomy would take me through a series of identity crises. I thought of myself as an exception, but I was wrong.

Like every serious woman athlete in America, I was to run into a set of obstacles that made the pentathalon look like a Sunday stroll. For openers, there's that skinny, pale model on the front cover of the fashion magazines—our feminine physical ideal. Instead of the long, lean muscles of Olympic sprinter Wyomia Tyus or the solid powerful strength of pentathlete Jan Svendsen, American women are told to cultivate the right color hair, glossed lips, eyes circled in silver-shadow blue, and a figure that's starved thin for firmness but not marred by a visible muscle. Women move in ways that reflect weakness and passivity as a standard of femininity. Women pose rather than stand, slink rather than stride. Most seem to move very tentatively, afraid of any assertive physical movements. Don't you dare move with strength and confidence if you are female. The ladylike crossed legs and folded hands and the model's stance, one leg in front of the other, are designed to make a woman look fragile and helpless, not free and ready to move.

Too great an emphasis on traditional feminine physical stereotypes puts a woman with athletic ambitions in a no-win situation. Either she is feminine and an athletic failure, or she's a sports success who finds her sexual identity threatened. Mannish, dyke, jock—I've heard that kind of name-calling leveled at women athletes for years. Exceptions only prove the rule. Robyn Smith is a jockey who poses for *Playboy;* but all jockeys are tiny—the physical requirements of her sport don't conflict with the standard female image. Olga Korbut is strong and feminine but in the highly balletic sport of gymnastics. But what about women hurdlers, or wrestlers, or baseball players? What about those women shot-putters? Can't we allow them to be strong, competent, and female? No wonder so many girls give up serious athletics for fear of developing "big muscles." No wonder so many parents grow concerned when their daughters become "overly involved" in sport. As if it's possible to be too strong, too vital, too alive.

But to give Dan Hruby credit, at least he gave a woman athlete some media coverage. At the time, most sportswriters acted as if women's athletics didn't exist. A woman's event was strictly three-line filler material—if the story was printed at all. Newspapers are doing slightly better today, thanks to heavy pressure from women's groups; and women athletes are taking sports coverage into their own hands with publications like *WomenSport*, founded by Billie Jean and Larry King. But daily coverage is still scanty, and too often sportswriters prefer to concentrate on a few stars. One year Chi Cheng was the only woman on the track; more recently Francie Larieu has been the trackwriter's darling. The media still fail to cover the whole field.

Media coverage is important because it draws fans, and fans mean money—the life blood of the current sports scene. If news coverage can nourish a sport (football's Superbowl is the prime example), then women's athletics has been starved to death. The poverty, and I mean poverty, of women's sports adversely affects the physical and mental health of 53 percent of the population. From kindergarten up, the physical development of girls and women is not considered of serious importance in capitalist America. This social norm results in bare bank accounts for women's sports. It also results in millions of females who have lost all touch with their own physical beings except as objects on view. Their bodies become passive, never actively involved in life.

As a student, an athlete, and later as a teacher of physical education, I saw firsthand how lack of money affects women's sports. I remember going to college track meets and sleeping overnight in the wrestling rooms or basketball courts of the schools we visited. Meanwhile, men's teams lounged around in comfortable local hotels. As a coach at California Polytechnic State University, I had a budget of $900 for the entire women's track program, less than one tenth of the money my male counterpart had to spend. In 1973–1974, when I taught at Oberlin College, the entire budget for women's athletics was $6,700 compared to $16,000 spent on men's football alone. (I should note that $6,700 represented a major achievement for athletic director Jack Scott, who was already under heavy fire for his effort to reform athletics at Oberlin. The previous year, the entire women's budget had been less than $1,000.)

Most men at some time in their lives have an opportunity to try their athletic abilities. They play the standard male sports, succeed more or less at some, and wind up with a pretty good idea of their athletic capacity. The high school football player becomes the knowledgeable fan of later years. His ticket money supports the sports activities of the next generation, and he probably maintains some athletic activity far longer than his wife.

Built upon this mass base, the male sports world looks like a pyramid. Young men are trained, coddled, and encouraged to rise through the ranks. Competition is tough, and at each step the best are selected and moved along until finally a few superstars stand at the pinnacle.

In comparison, because of the lack of facilities and coaching, few women have a chance to discover whether they have any athletic talent. As a result, women's athletics has no mass base, there is no middle range of steadily improving ability, and opportunities for sports stardom are few and far between. If anything, the women's sports scene looks like some kind of modern art painting—a flat line representing the nonathletic at the bottom and a tiny circle of serious athletes floating somewhere at the top. Patty Van Wolvelaere, a two-time Olympic hurdler, admits, "I've been number one hurdler in this country for years but I probably wouldn't be on top all alone if women's sports had decent channels for developing talent like the men have." Patty is a very able and dedicated athlete, and she expresses a concern shared by most of us. Lack of competition causes women's sports to lose credibility. Lack of credibility means that women's sports can't draw fans and money. Lack of money means that women athletes can't develop talent and reach a high competitive level. It's a vicious circle that's gone on too long.

As it stands now, every woman who decides to devote herself seriously to sport is a special case. Take me. According to my mom, I was born an athlete—I came out kicking. Mom was voted the top woman athlete at her high school in Paso Robles, California (just as I was given the same honor at Leigh High School, San Jose, some twenty-five years later). Her parents wanted a boy, and when they didn't have one after three tries, they contented themselves with a tomboy, naming her Glenn after her dad. Growing up on a ranch, she learned that women had to be tough and independent. Her dad hated "sissies." By the time Mom had me, she didn't think much of sissies either.

She married Bob Huey, jack-of-all-trades from carpentry to real estate to used car sales. Dad had played football, basketball, and baseball in high school. My parents decided to have only two children. My sister Margie came first, then a boy who died soon after birth. If my brother had lived, Lynda Huey wouldn't exist. Some psychologist probably could develop deep theories about me as a boy surrogate, daughter of a boy surrogate; I'd even be interested in hearing them. All I know is that I was brought up in a family where my physical accomplishments and interest in sports were praised and encouraged.

My dad taught me to run. At three I was racing him to the end of the block. He taught me to hit a ball and catch, and we developed a rivalry in tetherball that lasted for years. When I wasn't playing with Dad, I was trying to

The Huey family (I'm on the left)—Vallejo, California, 1948.

keep up with my acrobatic mother. She had me doing somersaults and cartwheels almost as soon as I could walk.

My family was more sports-minded than most, but I always craved all the activity I could get. I had energy to burn and could easily wear out my three or four closest girlfriends in our suburban neighborhood. I turned to the boys on the street to find playmates who could keep up with me.

"Beat ya to the corner!" someone would yell. I had to accept the challenge. I'd even give my challenger a head-start just to see how long it would take me to catch up. No matter what the sport, I learned to expect myself to be the best—always better than the girls and at least as good as the best guy.

My parents never subjected me to the "be a young lady" pressures that face most girls growing up. One day my third-grade teacher in a fit of prudery announced that girls could no longer play on the monkey bars because their panties showed. When I came home in tears, my mother sewed me colored panties to match my dresses. The other girls were grounded, but I could go on doing my two-legged circles and death drops as energetically as before.

Peer pressure for me to conform to sexual stereotypes really began in adolescence. I began reading those "How to be Popular" books and poring over each issue of *Seventeen* with more dedication than I ever gave to my schoolwork. Of course I wanted desperately to learn how to walk, sit, dress, and talk so that I could catch myself a respectable supply of boyfriends.

But my natural body energy cried louder than all those adolescent anxieties. I had to get up and *do*. I'd go shopping for material for a new dress, then stop on my way home to play football with the guys. I'd win an AAU (Amateur Athletic Union) gold medal in track then rush to get my hair done for the junior prom that night. I was a boy-crazy, popularity-conscious teenage girl who was trying to be an athlete at the same time.

I soon developed a split personality that split even further when I discovered that my best route to serious athletic activity was men. Since San Jose State didn't provide a decent track program for women, I charmed my way into workouts with the men. From 1967 to 1970 the Speed City Gang, the fastest group of runners ever assembled at one place at one time (including Tommie Smith, Lee Evans, John Carlos, and Billy Gaines) set up shop on campus. I ran and hurt and laughed with that super group of supermen almost every day for two years. They taught me the fine points of track, of life, of love.

It was an unforgettable time in my life, but I paid a heavy price for the memories. I became a male-identified woman. Soon I had as much machismo as the piggiest of the sports stars—and that's saying a lot. I ended up believing that anything a woman could do was insignificant compared to the joy of basking in the reflected glory of a Tommie Smith or a Wilt Chamberlain. My experiences with other "male" sports only intensified my MCP attitude. I made the California volleyball scene on the beaches and watched the women play supportive roles as the men controlled the game. I came to know football players—Redskins, '49ers, Eagles—and watched some of those men run through women like Kleenex.

I found myself with "male" attitudes toward women, but I also wanted to be able to play "female" to my heroes. I was caught in the dilemma of wanting to assert myself athletically, verbally, and sexually, but I also worried about the consequences of not conforming to the female norm. My self-esteem rose and fell like a roller coaster. I had to justify myself through male approval.

Too often I let social concerns take precedence over my athletic development. If Tommie Smith didn't show up at a workout, I'd be so disappointed I would cut my own effort in half. I even let a blowup in my love life sidetrack my athletic ambitions in the 1968 Olympic year. But my experience with male stars taught me a lot. I learned firsthand what it takes to be a great athlete. And I realized how far women's athletics has to change before women enjoy even a fraction of the opportunities available to men.

No, I never became a superstar, and at twenty-eight, I probably never will be one. I am a woman athlete with a good amount of natural talent who went through the system and wants to see it change. I've seen the mill that grinds up potential athletes: the understaffed and underfinanced school and college physical education departments, the second-rate and sometimes tyrannical coaching, the badly run sports events. Later, as a coach and physical education teacher I tried to buck the system that frustrated me. I've watched our best black athletes fight for their rights, and later, with Jack and Micki Scott at Oberlin College, I finally understood that the problems of women athletes are much the same, simply reflecting the second-class citizenship generally given to both blacks and women in this society.

Today the women's sports world is undergoing a revolution, and no one can be sure where it will lead. But I can already see seeds of change in the new toughness of my fellow women athletes, in the proud attitudes of the young girls I coach, and in myself. In the last few years I've developed the courage to claim myself; I've learned to establish friendships on an equal footing with the male superstars I once worshipped, and I've learned to set my own athletic goals and stick to them.

Through it all, my first love has been track. Several times in my life I've been discouraged by obstacles set up by society or by my own inadequacies and decided to give up the sport. But I learned quickly that I'm a true addict. I go through withdrawal every time I quit training. There's an actual physical hurt as my body craves exhausting exercise. During times of retirement, I notice that when I play a friendly game of racketball or work out in the weight room, I just don't feel right. The zing that's usually characteristic of my movements isn't there.

Then I go to a track meet, smell the liniment, see the concentration and intensity on the athletes' faces—and the next day I'm back on the track telling myself I'm there for an easy, nontraining, just-for-fun workout. Before I know what's happened, I'm running *hard* 220s. I see my shadow in full stride as I round a turn. "That's me right there," I tell myself. "How can I deny this part of me? How can I stop being myself?"

I yell "Track!" to a jogger plodding along and whiz by on the inside lane. Again, at last, I am powerful and in control. After the workout, I can feel that the way I carry myself has changed drastically. I look at my shadow again. My head is up and I'm walking with real sureness and physical pride. "This is what I've needed," I say to myself. "This is what I've missed."

I've always known that I am a woman. Equally important, I am an athlete. Today, I'm determined to be both.

in our school, the lust to win—all that emotion flooded over me as I made it happen.

Then, when it seemed as if the crowd could give no more, I took control again. My raised arms signaled the crowd that the moment was coming. They responded with a final peak of enthusiasm; I jumped high in the air and swooped down to a crouch to signal the cutoff. Instantly the shouting stopped. Wow. Dead quiet. You could hear a leaf fluttering down the bleachers. *I* performed that magic trick. I was in love with my own power.

"I'm *so* impressed!" I shout to the stands. "Yeah, we're gonna *kill* today."

Our team was on the field ready for the kickoff. I signaled to the song girls and the four other cheerleaders for our train formation. They relied on me—the spirit squad's only football expert—to tell them which way the kickoff was going. They lined up, each with one hand on the next girl's shoulder while the other hand cut giant circles in the air with a green pom-pom. The wheels of the train were moving.

"Goooooooooooooo," the crowd yelled. I took a ten-yard run, winding up for a cartwheel and a series of back flips until I heard the crowd roar. The ball was in the air. Our team was running forward. I turned to the field. I turned back to the crowd. As my parents and my friends' folks watched proudly from the stands, I had a job to do. It was up to our boys to carry that ball down to the goal line, but I led the battles that took place outside that grassy rectangle. I would exult in victory, weep in defeat. The football players were masters of the game; I was mistress of the crowd. I had no doubt that I was every bit as important as they were. I was every inch a star.

Of course the sports pages of the *San Jose Mercury* carried only half the story of each game. But my mom's home movies caught all the action. A few days after a game, the whole gang would gather at my house to see ourselves play

2

--->>> <<<---

We've Got the Spirit

L—E—I—G—H!
WE'VE GOT THE SPIRIT,
SO LET'S HEAR IT.
EVERYBODY STAMPEEEEDE!

And the crowd went crazy. More than 2000 fans ro
whistled, clapped their hands, and stomped their
Their throats burned from two straight hours of scr
ing, but on they screamed. I was pulling it out of ther
my cheerleader uniform, green sweater, and green
white pleated skirt, I was leading that vocal army a
loved every minute of it. All eyes were on me. I waved
hands frantically to work up the crowd; the noise kep
building to a frenzied pitch. I let the sound pour dowr
me from the stands. Love for the guys on the field, p

our leading roles. First, we'd watch Jim make a touchdown; then the camera would switch to my impromptu acrobatics on the sidelines. We'd see Gary break his leg, then zoom in on the cheerleaders in tears on the sidelines.

Becoming cheerleader or song girl was by far the most important thing a girl could do at Leigh High School. No other achievement, athletic or academic, compared. I figured that out as early as junior high school, when I went with my older sister Margie to her high school football games and fell in love with those heroines. Margie pointed to the field.

"Number 33, that's her boyfriend," she said, nodding at a blond cheerleader in front of us. "The girl next to her dates number 81."

My preadolescent brain had it all figured out. All you had to do was become a cheerleader and you had your choice of those gorgeous hunks on the football team. Love and status—a cheerleader owned them both, and I was willing to give up anything to be one. So in my freshman year of high school I gave up riding my bicycle to school (definitely an out thing to do). I gave up running around the park. I gave up skateboarding down the street. I gave up anything that was even borderline on the social acceptability scale. And while I ruthlessly forced myself to conform, I relentlessly "kissed up" to everybody. Walking down the hall, I smiled at literally everyone. I spoke a few words to this or that drip and smiled sweetly at the student body president. Everybody got a grin from me; I was politicking hard. Cheerleader elections were coming up fast and I *had* to win.

The cheerleader tryouts each spring were held in front of the entire student population. Each candidate performed a cheer, but the popularity politicking that had gone on all year was what really mattered. My turn: I did a routine complete with back flips, and I could tell that the crowd was impressed. I had to wait through the five slowest, most anxious hours of my life before I knew the results of the voting. My high school diary records the moment of victory.

May 29, 1962

I was so happy when I won cheerleader! This is the happiest day of my life. WOW! Did we SCREAM all through the corridors when we found out! It was so neat with everybody congratulating me and everything! I can't wait to get my outfit. I still can't believe it's for real. I'm just too happy!

Nothing else mattered. Witness my diary of October 23, 1962:

Kennedy's jazz about Cuba sure has me scared. I want to live. I just can't die before I really get to be a cheerleader and get to be totally IN.

Once I became a cheerleader, I was certified "in." I knew I could write my own ticket at Leigh High School. At last I was my own vision of the All-American girl. The school reinforced my self-image. Cheerleaders had special privileges. Cheerleading took precedence over the rest of my school activities. On Fridays before the game, I could wrangle an excuse from any class to prepare for the afternoon rally. The need to build school spirit was greater than my need to study.

All the cheerleaders involved themselves as much as possible in their roles, and I went one step further. I learned everything there was to know about the game of football. I hated to see a cheerleader have the fans yell, "We want a touchdown," right after one of our players had fumbled the ball. As long as I was a cheerleader, there would always be at least one person on the spirit squad who knew what was happening on the field.

We had status as the people closest to the men the crowd loved. The split end caught a touchdown pass and we mobbed him as he came off the field. Most of us became even more involved in the game by dating players. Each girl then had a champion who ran for her on the field. She cheered when he made a great play, wept when he was injured. With a boyfriend on the field, a cheerleader was as active a participant in the game as she could be short of actually playing.

I was determined to have one of the "good guys"—our name for the football players—as soon after I got my cheerleader uniform as possible. My devotion to my heroes was absolute. In my freshman year all I needed was a casual "hi" from number 31 on the football team and I was in love for months. I have to laugh at myself now, but when that same number 31 bought me a Coke one day I saved it—kept it in the deep freeze for over a year. Now, as a sophomore and a cheerleader, I knew I could turn my previous dreams into dates.

I remember the day when the head varsity cheerleader came running up to me to squeal that George Vierra was planning to ask me to the first big dance of the fall season. George, as halfback on the football team, guard on the basketball team, thirdbaseman on the baseball team, and student body president-elect, was the best of the good guys. I screamed with joy, yelled, swung around the nearest pole, and set eight consecutive new lifetime records in the vertical jump. Then I found out that George had been watching me. A bit embarrassing.

George didn't die laughing. Instead he asked me out for that Friday. Something must have gone right because soon I was spending Fridays, Saturdays, and every day with George. We became the campus First Family. After all, he was president. Bliss lasted for one year, until George left the Leigh High School scene and went to college. We vowed to be faithful. Then at the first party without

George, I found myself looking for a new hero. Players were prizes, part of the cheerleader mystique, and I was playing my role to the hilt.

As much as I loved my top-dog status, once in a while the political pressures cut into the fun. Once, when I traded in my player/boyfriends too often, I was warned that my fickle ways might cost me the next cheerleader election. Unfair! Football players were chosen for the team on the basis of pure talent; but cheerleaders (and I was one of the best) had to go through the annual uncertainty of a popularity contest, alias an election. More than once I wished I could be out on the field in shoulder pads and a football uniform just to have a little security.

Paul Hoch, in his insightful book *Rip Off the Big Game*, takes a negative view of cheerleaders.

> Football is America's number one fake masculinity ritual and the worshipping females are used to give the mock ritual its validity. More than that, the cheerleaders' tiny skirts and rounded sweaters also help inject the proper tension into the atmosphere. They are the modern day equivalent of the Vestal Virgins that the Romans maintained to bless their mass gladitorial spectacles.

Hoch's evaluation is based largely on pro football and would overstate the case at the high school level. At Leigh High the sex was certainly muted. Our uniforms were bulky: letter sweaters and bobby sox. Yet, looking back, I see that our football games were at least in part a masculinity ritual; football stars were considered the most attractive boys at the schools, and sex appeal was equated with athletic performance. The poor unathletic guy lost out in the social sweepstakes no matter what his other talents were.

Cheerleaders continually reinforced the male players in

For an athletically inclined high school girl, to become a cheerleader was the ultimate achievement. Here I am, leading my warriors into battle and executing a flip—and sampling my first taste of "stardom."

their positive role image. Men acted; we reacted. When a football player made a great play, cheerleaders rushed up to him, screaming and hugging. The players' achievements were tangible, recorded in the score—the number of yards gained, passes completed. Our triumphs were intangible. How do you measure spirit?

In my senior year, the school district officials tried to

introduce a measure of competition into cheerleading by awarding a spirit trophy to the best cheerleading squad in the league. Needless to say, we at Leigh High went all out for it. Everything was done with an eye to the judges. We even tried to stop any fun booing because that automatically deducted points from our spirit tally. But again, everything really depended on the team. With the winning team in the league, Leigh High cheerleaders didn't have too hard a time taking the spirit trophy.

But there were many games when we won the spirit award even though we didn't win the game, and those were the times that I felt I had really done my part for the school. Maybe the team hadn't won, but we had, out there on the sidelines. There was a feeling of futility though, to have given every single ounce of my help, sweat, and energy, and to know that I hadn't really been able to affect the outcome of the game. Even though we always preached that if we supported our team enough it could win, it made us feel helpless to know that we had done everything we could and the team still had lost.

Along with the sense of powerlessness about the outcome of the game, I felt a lack of personal recognition. I always felt somehow cheated when the spirit winner for that game was announced. All that the announcer gave was the final score. Had I, myself, earned any points with all of my backflips? Had any of my funny antics really helped? Nothing specific was ever credited to any of us, even though the guys could all read about their individual moments of glory in the next day's *San Jose Mercury*—even if they lost.

I have never felt that I was an atypical cheerleader. Almost every high school has a squad of girls like me. With few other outlets for positive recognition, many teenage girls still see their roles as spirit producers as the most important contribution they can make. The role of Super Fan is the one most socially acceptable and reinforced. Our supportive role for the football and basketball players is fairly symbolic of the marriage roles that are society's norms. The male is the real breadwinner, the one who goes into the *real* action, and the female cheers him on. Women's work is important, but it is always dependent on the male for its meaning.

As a cheerleader, I always loved the limelight, but that same experience set me up to accept a reflected limelight, a secondary role. I kept striving to be a star, yet I couldn't find—and no one wanted to help me find—my own route to starring achievement. Although I kicked, screamed, yelled, and hit heads all along the way, I knew deep down that men were the only legitimate heroes in the world and that my role was to worship their every move. If I hadn't lived that cheerleader role so successfully for three full years, I might not have tried so hard to recapture that high school Huey-in-Wonderland world that I had loved so completely—a world of fairytale unreality in which I had come to believe so strongly.

Sure, I had my glory, but at what price? I was now caught in the trap of always looking for heroes. My own accomplishments were meaningful only when seen in the shadow of a man's. If number 34 hadn't been out on the field, what would I have been? Obviously not a star. For a long while, I scorned women's athletic accomplishments and worshipped men's. I tried to continue my supportive role for male athletes by joining them. I was content to feel excitement by associating with the actors rather than having a full part in the action. For me, as for many women, the easiest path to glory was to accept the support-a-man cheerleader role.

3

-»» ««-

Pom-poms, Footballs, and
Spikes

November 22, 1963

John F. Kennedy, the president of the United States,
is dead. It's almost impossible to believe. These kinds
of things are read about in books but just don't happen. Johnson is president now and I really feel sorry
for him. He has a lot to overcome because most people
don't believe in him. I don't either.

John Kennedy's assassination was one of the few events
that ever took my mind off my world of high school football
games and pom-poms. Less than two weeks before his
death, my best friend Sue Swanson and I had decided that
we were part of the luckiest generation in America because
we could grow up with Kennedy as our president all

through our teenage years. And since no lesser politician could beat him in '68, our dream First Family would occupy the White House until we were twenty-one. In our eyes, John Kennedy was young, handsome, athletic, and strong—an idol. He appealed to everything inside me that wanted the world to be good.

The day of Kennedy's funeral was the first time I ever fasted. I don't know where the idea came from, but I knew that the day wasn't like any other and that it had to be treated differently. I felt as though I wanted to share physically a little of the pain. I didn't tell anyone what I was doing, but my mom seemed to understand. Ordinarily a fanatic on making sure I ate correctly, she offered me everything I normally would have eaten but didn't argue when I refused it. All the traditional "Turkey Day" games that were played the Thursday following the funeral were dedicated to his memory. That seemed appropriate to me because football was the most patriotic thing I knew. I thought the United States, Leigh High School, and Football were the three best things in the world.

My response to Kennedy's death was physical, my natural approach to the expression of sorrow or joy. Contrary to the myths of passive teenage girls, the sense of physical vitality dominated my life at that time, and I already had run into problems finding enough opportunities for the vigorous physical action I needed. I usually had to call on nearly all of my girlfriends to get enough exercise in one day. A couple of them would skateboard down to the school with me, where I'd hang around hoping somebody else would show up. Then while the first batch was still tired, I'd go down to the track and do some running by myself. Maybe later a couple more girls would show up and want to play some volleyball or basketball. It took at least two or three sets of girlfriends to wear me out.

Fortunately, one Sunday afternoon I stumbled upon my chance to get real exercise. Sue and I were wandering around when we discovered several of the "good guys" playing football on the field behind the school. Thinking they could embarrass us, the guys threw the ball in our direction. Not only did I catch the ball (I knew Sue wouldn't), but I threw a perfect spiral pass back to them 25 yards away. Instantly we were in the football game, and the guys were fighting over whose team I would join. It was heaven, and heaven was just beginning.

During the summer, six or seven guys would come over to my house nearly every day so we could jump on my back-yard trampoline and then go play football somewhere. We'd play two-hand touch down at the school, walking tackle football in the quad area, or knee football on my front lawn. It didn't matter what kind of football or even where we played; we all thrived on pitting our skills against each other's.

When some guys decided to have a football game or play in the waist-deep mud over at Guadalupe Reservoir, they took about nine or ten of their football buddies and me. A lot of my girlfriends regarded the guys' sports mania as if a love of physical activity came from a separate male approach to life. I jumped into the boys' sports eagerly just because boys were so much more vigorous and active than my sit-around-and-talk girlfriends. And I never felt that my inclusion with the boys was anything but a plus. I got to be with my favorite guys not only on Friday nights at the shows, but also on Saturday and Sunday afternoons— in the gyms or on the football field or in the parks. I was one of them for sports, but at the same time they allowed me to switch back to the "eligible girlfriend" status on date nights.

Most of my girlfriends seemed content sitting around discussing their love lives and plans for rallies. Once in a while some of them would jump into one of our football games for fun, but the nature of the game would change. Even though the guys and I flirted and grabbed each other when I was playing, we were still mainly interested in *playing*. With more girls involved, the game wasn't to be played, but to be played *at*.

Pam, my one girlfriend who had as much physical energy as I, had a mental block about being uncoordinated. Some of the other girls just giggled their way through the game. Every once in a while one of the girls would surprise everyone with a great tackle or a diving catch and I loved it, as did the guys. But most of the time, my girlfriends just acted cute and dropped the ball on purpose, while I grew disgusted with them. After all, the guys dug me and I did it right. Besides, I had seen these girls have flashes of aggressiveness in field hockey on our GAA (Girls' Athletic Association) team at school. In fact, about half of them were athletic and strong. Yet off the hockey field and in a casual pickup football game with the guys, they became instant klutzes. They could be a whiz with a hockey stick, charging down the field to score a goal, but they'd rather die than catch a pass and look like they knew what they were doing.

Being a loser just wasn't my style—one reason I found myself constantly at war with Leigh High physical education. Leigh High offered two versions of physical activity for girls—the normal physical education classes and the GAA. P.E. consisted of an hour a day of pseudo activity in different sports. It really didn't matter what sport was taught because the girls in the classes never did much more than dress in those blue shorts and white blouses and say "present" at roll call. I never worked up a sweat during a whole semester I was in one of those regular p.e. classes. My fellow students stood around, swatting half-heartedly at a wandering tennis ball now and then, more interested in fixing their hair and talking about their boyfriends. The main goal of the whole class seemed to be to avoid anything strenuous until the bell rang to end the torture.

The GAA was for more sports-minded girls, not that it consisted of the best athletes on campus. Many girls tried out for it because it was the last period and they wouldn't have to worry about ruining their hairdos early in the school day. Most of these girls got weeded out. Others, who had athletic talent, did not try out for GAA because in their social circle it was "out." GAA attracted most cheerleaders and song girls and did offer a higher level of activity than p.e. classes. It offered us a choice of two sports each quarter and an opportunity to compete with girls from other schools at the end of the term.

Naturally I wanted the best sports action I could get and tried out for GAA. To become a member I had to pass a physical fitness test—the 50-yard dash, softball throw, sit-ups, push-ups, shuttle drill, and a 600-yard run. I outscored every rival, so I knew I was going to be chosen. To my surprise, I wasn't.

It seems that I had an "attitude problem." I knew no one could complain about my performance on the athletic field —I was always on time, always ready to play, and always at my best. Rather, it was my manner that annoyed the women's gym establishment. I was a loud-mouthed, cocky, know-it-all who was not at all humble in her moments of glory. They seemed to want a robot wonder girl who would win everything, but not open her mouth when she saw things she didn't like. If I saw a better way to do things I said so, perhaps because I had already learned a skill my teacher didn't know, or sensed something about myself that defied her generalizations. In short, I was a discipline problem.

Yet even my discipline-minded teachers couldn't deny my athletic ability. After breaking virtually every school record in track and field during my regular p.e. class, I was invited to compete in the district track meet, even though I wasn't yet an official member of GAA. I won the 50-yard dash and anchored a totally unpracticed 440-yard relay team to a runaway first place. I played my politics right; I kept quiet during the entire meet and generally maintained a low profile. Three days later, the same teacher who had talked to me about my attitude problem told me I'd been accepted into GAA.

I soon found out that GAA was hardly the athletic big time. I quickly became the best player on its basketball team, but after learning the game from the guys, girls' basketball was a real drag. At that time, girls' rules had the court divided into two halves: guards and forwards played on opposite ends of the court, and only two players, rovers, were allowed to move freely up and down the court. A player could dribble the ball only twice before she had to pass. Now really—how could I do those crossover dribbles and fakes and jump shots I'd learned from the guys with a two-dribble rule? The game looked even more ridiculous when we played against the boys' varsity basketball team and then the freshman-sophomore team. Even Leigh's male basketball stars couldn't play much of a game following our rules. The reasoning behind the limited dribble rule was that girls were too frail to withstand the normal boys' game. But if we were considered too fragile on some occasions, our athletic abilities were recklessly wasted on others.

It still amazes me that I survived some of our ill-planned athletic contests. I remember one Saturday having to play five hockey games for our season championships. Well-seasoned athletes would have been taxed, and none of us knew anything about conditioning. We played 200 running —and I do mean running, then finally dragging and crawling—minutes of field hockey. That night a couple of the other cheerleaders and I had dates with our football-player boyfriends, but we knew we were too pooped to party. Our athletic boyfriends didn't understand. They had never played five games of anything in one day. Of course not. Each of their games was a major happening involving the entire student body.

Just about every aspect of the school program indicated

that girls' sports were less important than boys'. The home-made green shorts and white blouses that we wore took a real beating during the course of a year. They were our tennis uniforms, our hockey outfits, our basketball and track uniforms all wrapped in one. The boys received a different team uniform free for each sport, complete with name, number, and the Leigh High green and gold stripes. We had only one coach for each sport, but the guys had two or three. It was assumed that the guys needed the extra coaches to prepare them for the possible jump into college sports. Girls merely wanted to be entertained during our days at Leigh High. Moreover, the boys had legitimate officials controlling their games whereas our matches were officiated by women students from San Jose State College who were just learning to referee. They made almost as many mistakes in their calls as we made in our plays. We were frustrated because we did not have the proper physical skills or an environment conducive to our best play.

On rainy days, we learned that our volleyball game wasn't nearly as important as our coaches had led us to believe. The football team told us they needed the gym to continue their practice for the big game coming up Friday, so we docily moved out and let them have the facilities. After all, it was more important for them to be ready on Friday to play the big game against Saratoga High than it was for us to be ready to go play a mediocre volleyball game against some of our competitors. The school status was based on the boys' athletic teams, not the girls'. Everyone knew that Leigh High and Saratoga High were battling for the football league championship, but who cared if the Leigh High girls' basketball team beat Del Mar 24–10 and that I scored twelve points?

All the cheerleaders went to the boys' sports banquet to grin as our boyfriends got their trophies. My junior year I won a round of applause when I got the "prettiest statistician" trophy from the boys' baseball team. The next day I saw my name in the paper for receiving the award, but the press didn't note that I had won two legitimate athletic awards of my own only the week before. At the GAA sports banquet—which hardly got the same attention—I won both the Outstanding Basketball Player award and the Outstanding Track Athlete award.

Naturally, most of the girls internalized the message of their second-rate status. They believed that it was more important to be somebody's prettiest bookkeeper than to outrun their opponents at a girls' track meet. I remember being caught off guard one day by one of the song girls. She got a head-start on me in a practice windsprint and I had to run 100 percent to catch her. She was almost as fast as I was, and it surprised me. I never would have guessed; she concealed her talent so well.

"Why don't you come on my AAU relay team in the Cow Palace next month?" I asked her. "We need one more really fast girl." "No," she said. "My calves are too big already. They might get bigger."

Had girls' sports been given any support from the rest of the school or the community, it might have been worth the price of the muscular calves to have taken part. But this particular song girl knew that she could get a lot more attention with a pom-pom in her hand than with spikes on her feet.

I wanted both the pom-poms and the spikes. But for a long time I never felt I could have both. When my teachers noticed in my freshman year that I was especially fast, they encouraged me to train with a local AAU team. They knew that the school system simply didn't offer enough competitive opportunities to do me much good. When I practiced one day with the AAU girls I learned that I was already faster than any of them. I was tremendously encouraged until I returned to school and sat down for a long talk with my p.e. teacher, Miss Van Pelt.

"Running at that level of competition won't be easy, you

know," she said. "You will have to train at least two hours a day. You won't be able to set foot in a swimming pool during the competitive season, and you'll have to stay away from that trampoline you have in your backyard."

"What about cheerleading?" I asked.

"I really don't think you'd have time for cheerleading if you decide to run with this track team. It will take every minute that you aren't involved with school."

Everything around me said that leading cheers at rallies and making spirit posters was far more important than running around in circles. Miss Van Pelt made me feel that I was required to make an irrevocable choice between being a normal young woman or a single-minded, monkish track athlete. She had taken enough interest in me to suggest track training, but her proposition was full of "can't do's" when I wanted to hear the "cans" and the "do's." I doubt that a male coach would have offered training to a boy student in quite the same way. Male athletes are expected to lead normal lives; their athletic skills only bring them more social approval. Of course, Miss Van Pelt couldn't paint the visions of of athletic glory that a football coach uses to persuade a prospective quarterback because there was no status attached to girls' sports.

I had just made my breakthrough into the high school social world by becoming a cheerleader; the weather was hot, and the swimming pool looked inviting. I picked up my books and said to Miss Van Pelt, "Thanks, but no thanks," and walked away.

But eventually track was a sport I couldn't refuse. One evening the summer before my senior year I saw a group of girls running around the track that surrounded the Leigh High football field. A tall husky man with white-blond hair, Duke Drake, stood in the center of the field giving them directions. I went out to him and boldly announced that I could run a 50-yard dash in 6.2 seconds—an impressive claim, especially for an untrained athlete. I don't know whether Drake believed me, but he invited me to train with his team the next weekend.

Drake coached the SCVGTC, the Santa Clara Valley Girls' Track Club, the AAU club Miss VanPelt had urged me to join 3 years earlier. The Amateur Athletic Union is the governing body for amateur sport in America and organizes competition from the local to the national and international levels in many sports, including track and field. With the exception of a few schools and colleges, the AAU offered women track athletes their best opportunity for training. As at Leigh High, most male athletes had adequate facilities at their schools and remained within the high school and college system until they had finished their four years of college eligibility. Then if they wanted to continue competing, they turned to an AAU team. Women, however, needed the AAU to provide a decent standard of competition. I was enthusiastic about Santa Clara and wrote in my diary,

June 30, 1964

Am I pooped!!!! My first workout with the Santa Clara Valley track team and Mr. Drake gave me a pair of spike track shoes and said I did a real good job. I feel that maybe I'll eventually be able to get GOOD.

Those were the dirtiest, raggediest, nastiest looking pair of cloddy, heavy track shoes in existence, but they were the first pair of spikes I had ever seen and I loved them. Wow! To feel that "ka-runch" as the spikes bit into the dirt. And to watch those funny little marks I left in the track.

What awe I felt toward those shoes. They proved that I was a *real* runner now, even though I had no idea what being a real runner meant. I had a long way to go before I knew what it was like to have a finely tuned set of legs and to be in shape. For me, running was still pure fun; I would eagerly put my natural speed on the line against anyone else's ability.

Sally Griffin, a girl on the Santa Clara team I had beaten in a race several years earlier, had been training with the Santa Clara Valley Girls' Track Club for three years and could now outrun me. Tall, lean, and good-looking, she was the first attractive role model I met in track. No matter when I talked to her, she was either on her way to or from a track meet on the other side of the country or the other side of the world. Track seemed like the most exciting thing I could do, especially since Coach Drake hadn't said a word about my having to give up swimming or trampoline. Olympic visions danced in my head. Why had I let myself be talked out of this before? It made me angry to think that I had lost out on three potentially good years of track competition.

At that point I still didn't know anything about getting in shape. I trained with Drake's team on Saturdays, and I nearly threw up after every practice. I was faster than almost everyone on the team in a one-time, all-out sprint, but they were in better shape and soon wore me out. Coach Drake suggested that I run at least fifteen minutes a day to help me keep up with their Saturday workouts. But even when I tried to take the time, I didn't know what to do in those fifteen minutes. Sometimes I went to the track and felt hopelessly lost without my team there, and often wound up doing nothing.

My natural speed, however, enabled me to do quite well in the northern California AAU meets, and I became a known sprinter in the 14–17 age group. Then the annual GAA track meet approached. Under school district rules, I couldn't compete in it because I was running for an AAU team. But I had almost single-handedly won the district track meet for Leigh High School during both my sophomore and junior years, and if the team could win the trophy just one more year, the school would get to keep the perpetual trophy. I knew that if I ran Leigh could win, but that the school didn't stand a chance if I was ineligible. I decided to quit the SCVGTC two months before the track meet, thus making myself eligible passing up at least five meets on the AAU circuit.

I couldn't wait for the GAA track meet. Most of the guys on campus had been hearing about me running in the San Francisco Cow Palace indoor meet that year and were planning to come to the GAA meet to see if I was as good as my reputation. I had a brand new pair of spikes, and the boys' coach had taken time to work with me on my start, so I was ready to break any and all school records. Then I made the mistake of mentioning my excitement about my spikes to my p.e. teacher.

"That's very nice, dear," she replied, "but you won't be able to wear those spikes. We decided not to allow spikes at the meet because most of the girls don't have them."

"But so what?" I said. "Most of them aren't as fast as me either. Does that mean that I can't run because I'm better?"

"Lynda, why do you always have to cause problems? We decided among all the coaches at all the schools that we won't allow spikes. That's that. Period."

I wore tennis shoes in that track meet. I won every race I ran.

4

⇢≫ ≪⇠

A Course in Frustration

"Physical education" was the first thought that popped into my mind when the San Jose State College registrar's office demanded to know what I wanted to do with the rest of my life. I chose p.e. for lack of a better answer. At the time, I was suffering from a bad case of culture shock. The athletic–social star of the Leigh High senior class had just become a San Jose State freshman—another number in the registrar's computer. I knew I was somebody special, but the thousands of new faces I passed each day on the crowded campus didn't seem to care. In the midst of my confusion, p.e. promised to be a continuation of high school athletics, and I desperately wanted to find some familiar ground on that unfamiliar campus. So I wrote "Physical Education/French/English" in the slot labeled "major" on my #2 IBM card. When my assignment to the physical education department came through, I thought, "Good as anything else."

I was wrong. Not that I'd joined an inferior department. To the contrary, the San Jose State College physical education program was considered one of the best in the California State College system and possibly one of the best on the west coast. SJS had an outstanding reputation for athletics and had already gathered together some of the leading track athletes in America. Certainly, many of my women professors were hard working and well educated.

Yet, in 1965, women's physical education at SJS seemed custom-tailored to undermine any woman of high energy and serious athletic ambition. The program—not at all atypical of women's p.e. programs then and today—suffered from a limited range of opportunities and low athletic expectations for its students. The SJS men's p.e. department had a variety of programs—for men who wanted to learn to teach basic skills as well as for those who prepared to coach high-level competitive athletics. The separate, but not at all equal, women's p.e. department offered training on only the most elementary level of sports. Women were trained to teach, not compete or coach. I knew almost immediately that I was in the wrong place, but there was nowhere else to turn. Inside or outside the physical education department, SJS did not provide training and support for the woman athlete who wanted to excel. As a result, I became a discipline problem—and a case study in frustration.

My first class in p.e. taught me that it had nothing at all to do with athletics. My disenchantment began from the moment I met my fellow students. I recorded my reaction in my diary on September 27, 1965:

"I'm feeling like an out-of-it type freshman. It's all because of my p.e. class. There are four neat girls in it, but they're all Sorority Sals. The rest of the girls are typical p.e. majors . . . Hercs! I sure hope it gets better."

My p.e. classes made the woman–athlete dichotomy clear for the first time. At Leigh High I managed to combine both roles successfully, but the SJS p.e. students made a personality split seem inevitable. The sorority girls were at first glance my natural allies. They were the campus leaders, the best-looking, most popular girls around. True, their athletic abilities usually were not impressive; in gymnastics, none of them could do anything much tougher than a forward roll. They seemed more worried about their pancake makeup or their false eyelashes than about learning a new physical skill. Still, I considered them attractive and for a short while wanted to be one of them. Sports were only half my life, and a Kappa Kappa Gamma or Kappa Alta Theta sorority pin seemed the key to success on the social scene. Unfortunately (or fortunately, as it turned out), social life was expensive, and I couldn't ask my parents to foot the bill.

I naturally would have turned to the more athletically inclined women in the department, but the "Hercs," as I called them, were the worst male chauvinist pig's description of a woman athlete. Overweight and mannish, they had neither the bodies nor the minds of real athletes. It looked to me as if they had decided to pursue careers in p.e. because life didn't offer them any better alternatives.

My feelings of alienation increased when I considered my teachers, theoretically my role models. Some were wonderful women—Leta Walter, the hockey coach, and Carol Luther, track coach, two of the kindest and most supportive women I've ever met. Carol had a fine southern sense of humor and a relaxed approach to teaching. She realized her limitations as an advanced track coach and generously allowed me to plant myself under the direction of Bud Winter, coach of the men's track team. Even though I traveled and competed for her team, Carol never let her ego get in the way of her student's growth.

But these women were exceptions. Most of my teachers were hardly the types to impress a man-conscious freshman. And I learned that my worst suspicions were true: only two of the twelve physical education professors were married. At age eighteen I found that frightening. I thought back to my junior high and high school p.e. teachers; I realized that all of them were "Miss." Physical education seemed to make women off limits to men, and I certainly didn't want to be quarantined.

My doubts about continuing as a p.e. major deepened as I heard rumors that the department was filled with lesbians. Believe it or not, naive freshman that I was, I didn't even know what a lesbian was. When I found out, I was horrified. Today, I couldn't care less about the sexual orientations of others, and I believe we all must be free to conduct our sex lives as we choose. But at the time, my attitude toward sex was bound by very narrow prejudices, and, although those rumors were never confirmed, I certainly wasn't delighted by the departmental image.

The p.e. department seemed to overreact to its bad press. Our professors, perhaps determined to prove our "femininity," insisted that all p.e. majors maintain a lady-like appearance at all times. Women p.e. majors were required to wear skirts on campus, whereas women in other majors were free to dress as they pleased. I knew how to dress as well as any sorority sister, but often I didn't want to bother. The casual jeans and T-shirt outfits many of the other girls wore looked appealing. After I'd studied all night and barely dragged myself to a midterm, I was in no mood to fix my hair and put on a dress. So I didn't. Many times I was caught crawling through the corridors in a football jersey and jeans. I became an expert at ignoring the dirty looks of my instructors. And unfortunately for all concerned, the dress code didn't help the p.e. department's reputation one bit. The fat plain girls in p.e. looked a lot worse in white socks, tennis shoes, white blouses, and straight skirts than they would have looked in a nice pair of pants. And given the popular attitudes toward women athletes, all the Diors in the world wouldn't convince some people that a woman athlete could really be a woman.

The discovery that physical education had negative sex appeal soon frightened the sorority girls away. First the Kappa Alpha Theta left to go into art. Then the Kappa Kappa Gamma and Alpha Phi switched to more socially acceptable majors. The Sorority Sals resolved the woman–athlete dilemma by declaring themselves women and gave up potentially rewarding careers in sport.

My reaction was different. Although for a while I seriously considered changing majors, in the end I decided to stick with p.e. But I told myself that although I was a p.e. major on paper, I didn't have to be one of *them*. If most of the girls in my classes hardly knew men existed, I'd show them that I had a few in my life. Whenever I walked around campus, with a particularly gorgeous guy, I made sure we strolled through the Physical Education and Recreation building and were seen by fellow students. Whenever I'd wear a crazy T-shirt to hockey practice, I let my teammates know that the shirt came straight off the back of an irresistible Italian pole-vaulter. When a date at a party told me that "sports make women masculine"—a not uncommon comment—I'd offer myself as proof to the contrary. "You asked me out, didn't you?" I'd say.

In a way I was just as defensive as my p.e. teachers with their round-collar blouses and dull pleated skirts. I overstressed my own attractiveness to conquer the self-doubts that other people planted in my mind. I'm convinced now that the need to prove myself as a woman developed in the SJS physical education department and was a major cause of my free-wheeling sexual behavior later in life. Whichever way we tried to handle the prejudice that separated "woman" from "athlete," the Sorority Sals, the Hercs, and I all suffered. Fighting against the prejudice made it very difficult for us to develop a comfortable and positive attitude toward ourselves as athletes.

I soon learned, however, that the antiwoman image of the p.e. department wasn't its only problem. Women's physical education was accorded low status by almost every standard. For example, p.e. was not considered an academic major. Students in other majors did not need a minor to meet teacher education requirements, but we did. I took English, amazed that plowing through my p.e. courses on anatomy, kinesiology, and biology was not adequately "academic." Apparently the science of training young people to develop strong, healthy bodies is not deemed sufficiently demanding by ivory tower standards, and p.e. majors are constantly trapped in the "dumb jock" stereotype.

But women p.e. majors weren't even considered jocks. The men's physical education department trained important athletes and stars on the campus, but being a female athlete counted for nothing. I was a female athlete with the same cockiness and pride in my physical accomplishments as a man, and many times I wished that I could major in men's p.e.

Many of the other women physical education majors weren't athletes at all. Overweight and uncoordinated, they appeared to lack even average athletic ability. And the difference between women's and men's p.e. wasn't entirely physical. The male athletes I knew were always dead serious about their competitive endeavors. On the other hand, the women p.e. majors seemed more concerned with the social and recreational benefits of physical activity. A superlative performance on the hockey field wasn't as important as a pleasant cookies-and-punch social hour with the opponents afterwards. I hated those functions. I never could get my competitive spirit turned off so quickly, and I hated having to make social conversation with a team that moments before had defeated us. I wanted a chance to go to the locker room and cool off in a shower before I had to be nice to my opponents. And I resented the implication of our mandatory parties—the notion that the game didn't matter.

The cookies-and-punch mentality was typical of the physical education department's approach to sports: don't worry who wins or loses; don't worry whether you play well or not. But I worry. As an athlete my temper is volatile, and I am outraged when my teammates don't take a contest as seriously as I do. As a result, tears, frustration, and anger were constants in my college sports career. No one else seemed willing to respect fully the legitimacy and importance of the athletic effort.

While athletics were downgraded, the physical education course of study was presented with an incredible defensiveness. My p.e. teachers seemed to try continually to prove that theirs was a legitimate topic for study. Instead of preparing us to teach sport, they prepared us to battle with all the people who would challenge our choice of p.e. as a field of study.

The department seemed to emphasize form rather than content, teaching by the book rather than getting results. In the methods of teaching physical education class, for example, much time was spent learning to take roll, to conduct drills, to maintain discipline. No one seemed interested in building superior female athletes. Even though we were taught to encourage students to experiment with their physical abilities and to proceed at their individual paces, I always felt that my teachers didn't practice what they preached. I was constantly held back.

The activity classes, where theoretically we learned the skills we later would teach, were disappointing. In my beginning gymnastics class I became the class demonstrator; I knew all the stunts on the lesson plan because I had been doing them since junior high school. When I wasn't

demonstrating I'd be so bored in a class that I'd start enter-
taining myself with harder stunts that I'd mastered years
before.

"Would you like to join us, Miss Huey?" the instructor
would ask. "Or do you think that you're too good for us?"
How I would have loved to give her an honest answer. Not
only did I think I was too good to join them, I knew I was.

My instructors insisted on elaborate safety precautions,
yet required that I go to class rather than properly treat a
foot injury I received on the basketball court. I remember
leaping up for a rebound and coming down on the side of
my foot. Suddenly I was lying there on the floor with a
crowd around me, while my teachers managed to get some
ice cubes out of the women's faculty lounge. They made an
icepack to prevent swelling. Then they aimed me toward
my next class. I sat in pain while my instructor talked about
dance in ancient Greece. Instead, I should have been down
at the health center getting a proper icing to prevent the
hemorrhaging that was rapidly turning my foot into a
kaleidoscope of purple, greens, and blues. I know that no
men's sports coach would treat his athlete's injury so casually—at least no coach who wanted to keep his job.

All through my physical education classes I felt reined
in, held down. Whenever I saw a new physical skill demon-
strated, I wanted to try it immediately. At last, a challenge!
But our instructor always insisted that we go slowly. Somebody might get hurt. We proceeded to learn each new skill
with such mind-deadening caution that I didn't have any
interest left in trying by the time we were ready to make
the attempt.

I think many women remember similar experiences with
their physical education during their high school and college careers. Those old blue gym shorts could be a symbol
for athletic regimentation and mediocrity. Take girls'
push-ups, for example. Most young women have not developed much upper body strength, and p.e. classes cater to

this weakness. Girls learn to lift their weight from the knees rather than to lift the whole body in normal, full-length push-ups. But why should physical education teachers accept, indeed encourage, this second-rate performance? Why not set strength as the goal and help women toward it?

Physical education as it was taught to me was not directed toward developing real women athletes. The underlying message of p.e. seemed to be: keep a young woman's expectations about her physical self low. Teach her about fitness by telling her to lose fat and be slim rather than urging her to be strong, vigorous, and proud of her body. Make her feel uncomfortable if she's well defined muscularly. Teach her to respect athletic mediocrity in herself and others. If she tries to excel or speaks out when she finds a shortcoming in the program, tell her she's a discipline problem.

By the time I graduated from the San Jose State p.e. department I had lost interest in teaching physical education. Later, working on my own and with a few inspiring fellow teachers, I learned that physical education can escape that mind- and body-deadening regimentation and emphasis on mediocrity and methodology that for years has caused high school girls to lose interest in sports. Certainly, no one loved the challenge of strenuous physical activity more than I did, but just a few weeks as a student of physical education left me completely frustrated. The p.e. teachers made it seem impossible to be successful as both a woman and an athlete. If I wanted to do both, I had to strike out on my own.

5

→》》《《←

Discovering that "Natural High"

Thwack. A damn wiffle ball right in the head. Now who do I know here who would have thrown that at me? I was at the Santa Barbara relays the spring of my freshman year in college to root for the San Jose State men's team; but the only two guys I knew on the team were already out on the track warming up for their distance race. I looked around and at the end of the bench sat a long loping black male decked out in a pair of dark, dark sunglasses and a big thirty-two-tooth grin. I smiled back.

Next thing I knew, the grin had joined me down on the grass where I lay stretched out on my coat watching the meet. The grin had a gold tooth smack in the middle of it and the long legs looked familiar. I knew I had seen this man on the track during some of my workouts, but I couldn't come up with a name.

"What 'choo doin' besides watching the track meet, junior?" gold tooth and dark glasses wanted to know.

"Watching the track meet," I cleverly answered. "How about you?"

"Watchin' you."

"And throwing wiffle balls," I said.

He didn't have time for a denial. The SJS assistant coach, Don Geyer, called to him, "Better start warming up, Tommie, the 880 relay goes off in thirty-five minutes."

He was gone before I had time to glance back at the grin who now had a name—Tommie. I wondered if he was Tommie Smith. I'd heard we had a super sprinter on our team by that name but I didn't know anything about him. I stood next to the assistant coach as the relay started. Tommie was running the last, or anchor, leg on the relay as SJS faced the University of Southern California and the University of California at Los Angeles, our biggest competitors.

"If Tommie can just get the baton within 5 or 6 yards of the other guys, he can win it for us," the coach said.

Hey, this guy must be pretty good, I thought. He was. A bad handoff early in the race cost the SJS team a lot of ground. When Tommie took the stick, he was in fifth place, about 10 yards from the leader, Norm Jackson. Tommie snatched that baton and turned those dark glasses straight ahead in what had to be the most exciting display of broken field running around a turn I have ever seen.

His anchor leg of that 880 relay wasn't run in lanes, so he had to duck and dodge bodies and flying elbows all the way. He blew by Larry Questad from Stanford and Dwight Middleton of USC. As he came off the turn, he lifted his shoulders and head with real purpose, leaned a bit further forward, and dug that long smooth stride of his even deeper into the track. He hit the tape well ahead of the field.

As I think about it, the physical education department

practically drove me into Tom's life. Soon after I arrived in the p.e. department I wanted out. Since p.e. failed to provide much of a focus for my college experience, I lived in a state of confusion and doubt. The only solid base I had found was track. Again, my diary:

January 25, 1966

Wish I knew what I wanted to do long range, not just one week in advance, but with my LIFE. It's the only one I have and as far as youth goes, it's just about up. The only thing that got me out of my horrible mood today was running down at the track. Thank God for exercise that clears the brain.

I channeled most of my excess energy into whatever track activity I could find, and that was too little. San Jose State had a widely respected men's track program complete with coaching, top-quality facilities, and regularly scheduled meets on the college circuit, but the women's program was very poor. Women's coach Carol Luther, competent as she was in many phases of athletics, would admit that track was not her forte. The women's track team had its first practice about a month before the only meet of the year, so obviously the women did not have an ongoing program of conditioning or competition. Not that San Jose State was particularly sexist; the absence of regular competitive sports for women was typical of colleges in the mid-sixties.

I continued my association from high school with the Santa Clara Valley Girls' Track Club and ran in AAU meets. But Coach Drake had left, and the club had a new coach and a new training site. I could work out there only once a week. But my college class schedule left me with free daytime hours, a luxury compared with my crowded high school schedule, and I started using the three-hour breaks to work out. I found that running alleviated a lot of the frustration the rest of the day produced.

One day I was a bit later than usual for my workout and noticed a lot of men on the SJS track. I tried to sneak away without being noticed, but an acquaintance from high school spotted me and soon I was working out with him and another distance runner on the team. My workout was so much easier that day, that the next afternoon I went out to the track a little later again. Soon I was working out with the men's track team every day.

I needed all the help I could get. At the San Francisco Cow Palace Indoor Meet that year, I had managed to help pull in a third place for our sprint relay team despite the fact that I was clumsy on the small wooden track and had not yet learned to run the sharp banked turns. Again, my natural talent triumphed over lack of coaching.

Bud Winter, the SJS men's track coach and former U.S. Olympic team sprint coach, allowed me to join in the technique work and interval training with the male sprinters. But working out with the men's team had its limitations. I had to take whatever help I could manage to get, and if I wanted to learn a new event, I was strictly on my own. The previous summer I had won third place in the Western U.S. Championships in the long jump with a leap of 17 feet 1 1/4 inches. (Not bad for an untrained athlete—a leap of 18 feet at that time would have made me a national caliber long jumper.) I was interested in continuing this event, but I had no one to coach me. Hurdling was the same story: no coach.

The male athletes were in a different position. By the time they reached college, they already had learned the basic track and field skills, and they spent their time refining their technique and conditioning their bodies. After four years of high school track, I still knew next to nothing and had to start learning the fundamentals of the sport. I had plenty of teachers in the sprints, so even though I had pentathalon dreams, hurdle dreams, and long-jump dreams, I always woke up doing high knee drills with the sprinters. I was so grateful to be included in a high level of athletics that it was easy for me to let track become one of the main supports in my life. My attraction to Tommie Smith, who also lived for track, seemed like the most natural thing in the world.

Tommie was a shy, complex man with a fierce dedication to his sport. The future Olympic superstar was born in Ackworth, Texas, one of twelve children of a sharecropper. After the farm boss nearly killed Tommie's dad one night in a fight, the family packed their belongings and headed west to Lemoore, California. There they barely eked out a living picking cotton. Tommie remembers going to school and watching the other kids eat lunch while he went hungry. Later, as a world record holder in college, Tommie got along on a steady diet of peanut butter sandwiches.

"Why didn't you come eat with me?" I asked years later when I'd learned of his poverty in college. "I would have fed you."

"You know how it is," he shrugged.

No, as a child of the middle class, I didn't know, and Tommie Smith, who walked with the military bearing he had acquired in his ROTC training, wasn't telling. He kept his hurts to himself and hid his shyness behind big black horn-rimmed sunglasses. They were originally prescription glasses. By the time Tommie lost that pair, he had become addicted to the pleasures of looking out when no one could look in, and he continued to wear nonprescription sunglasses, even during his races.

That pair of shades became his trademark, and he gave the press a million reasons why he wore them. He would tell one reporter that the shades kept the sun out of his eyes so he wouldn't squint and tighten his facial muscles, which tightened all his neck muscles, which tightened his arm and shoulder muscles, and so on all the way down that lanky frame. Another reporter heard that Tommie wore his shades to block his peripheral vision so he could avoid being distracted by his competitors. All the reasons he gave the press probably were valid in one way or another, but I think that the explanations were invented after Tommie had grown too comfortable hiding behind the shades to give them up.

Not that Tommie "Jetgear" Smith had any reason to hide when it came to track. Jetgear was the nickname given him by sportswriters who had seen him run. He did seem to have a different set of equipment than other sprinters. He was 6′3″ and had wiry arms and licorice-stick legs—185 pounds of raw speed. When Tommie headed down the track and stuck his head out a little further than normal, signaling a change of gears, you knew a record was coming. His knees would start pumping so high they almost hit him in the chest, and those lower legs would reach out further than you would believe possible. He was a beautiful runner —with incredible fluidity, evenness of stride, power, and strength.

Tommie knew exactly what he was doing, and he taught me the basic components of a good workout: the warm up, the technique work, the interval training, and the warm down. Before Tommie, I had no real insight into which workout routine was suitable for early season and which for midseason, which drills built endurance and which built speed. I only had a repertoire of two or three workouts learned from Duke Drake. I would go down to the track with my transistor radio for company and try to discipline myself to do whichever workout I thought might be appropriate. Tommie, though, was extremely business-like during practice. The key to each workout was a series of sprint drills developed by Bud Winter. Bud's drills were the secret of the distinctive San Jose sprint style. Most runners had to fight for the high knee lift and fluidity of movement that seemed so natural in Tommie, so Bud made form drills mandatory in each workout, requiring his sprinters to exaggerate every point of good technique so that good form would become second nature, even under the pressure of competition.

Each day Bud lined us up in two rows and put us through our paces. "High knees," he shouted, and I ran with my partner 30 to 40 yards down the track trying to keep my knees as high as possible. At Bud's shout of "fore-leg reach," I tried to match strides with my partner. I lifted my knees first, then the forelegs, trying to lengthen my stride as far as possible. The next phase was arm action. I stood in place, pumped my arms vigorously, then ran down the track continuing the powerful arm action. I was amazed to see how much my speed would increase with improved arm action.

"Forward lean," Bud would order. I lifted up onto my toes, then leaned forward until I had to take a step to keep from falling. At the moment when I was about to lose my balance, I was at the proper sprinting angle, and I tried to maintain the same forward lean throughout a sprint. In "Run tall," I held my body high, chest out, trying to feel as light on my feet as possible. Bud told us to imagine that someone had attached a string to our heads pulling us up; I could always feel that string and get lighter on my feet almost automatically.

After we'd worked on the specific points of the sprint technique, Bud told us to stop, shrug our shoulders a few times, swing our arms around in circles, and let them hang. Even though a sprinter in a race contracts some muscles as vigorously as possible, other muscles are not being used and must be relaxed. Muscles work in antagonistic pairs: when one contracts, its antagonist must relax to allow the contractor maximum power. Without relaxation, unnecessary movements can emerge in a sprinter's stride and slow her down. And nonworking muscles that are not fully relaxed can exert a pull that essentially puts a brake on the muscles that are attempting to work. As muscles begin to contract and relax alternately with precision, sprinting becomes more efficient. Beginning sprinters were always surprised to hear Bud shout "relax" in the midst of a race, but they soon understood that relaxation was the key to the Winter sprint style and the source of the incredible fluidity of runners like Tommie Smith.

The sprint-form drills helped train our muscles in the precise movements they would be required to make in competition. A beginning runner often forgets form in high-pressure situations, but gradually, through constant reinforcement of the proper movement patterns, that efficient sprinter's style emerges even in the most aggressive, competitive circumstances.

Tommie and I couldn't do that part of the workout together because his stride was much longer than mine. I usually did my knee lifts and arm action drills with Bob Griffin, who, at 5′6″, was more my size. Although Bob could beat me easily when he ran all out, we could almost match strides when we worked at this slower pace.

After the form drills came interval training. Mondays we ran ten 110-yard windsprints. Tuesdays our program was five 220s. Wednesdays either three 352s or three 330s. Thursdays our routine varied—either 220s or 110s, the shorter sprint if we had a meet scheduled that weekend. We had workouts on Fridays only if there was no competition on Saturday since Bud believed in a day of rest before a meet. Before a high-quality performance can be achieved, the muscles need a day to get rid of waste products that accumulate during hard contractions and to store up needed nutrients for an all-out effort.

Suddenly my workouts had a framework that made sense. I was learning when, why, and how to prepare for a race. I joined Tommie as often as I could for interval training. When we ran 110s, Tommie gave me a 20-yard head-start so he would have to run hard to catch me before I crossed the white pegs that were set up around the track every 110 yards. That totally smooth runner working beside me was awesome. I saw his knees lifting almost to his chest and smiled—what a gorgeous runner.

The time spent talking between sprints was as much an education for me as the actual exercises. Tommie and I often talked about how we felt, what parts of our bodies felt light and strong, what parts were giving us trouble. I was reassured to learn that even the supermen of track and field had human bodies with normal aches and pains. And instead of ignoring my injuries, I learned how to take care of a temperamental sprinter's legs and feet.

At first I thought that Tommie, a Superman, never hurt the way I did during a workout. Everything he did seemed so effortless that I didn't give him much credit for working hard. As I came to know him better and to be familiar with his mannerisms, I learned to detect subtle signs of pain. The area just under his eyes would turn almost beige as the chocolate color of his skin drained out. His eyes would squint slightly—the more squint, the more pain. Tommie's success wasn't merely a matter of natural speed as some people preferred to think. This fast man's speed was a result of talent, incredible effort, and a willingness to pay the price in pain.

Understanding Tommie's effort helped me increase my dedication. After a hard sprint together, we'd stand together at the finish line bent over and gasping for air. "Come on," he'd say if I took too long catching my breath. "Don't let it control you. You take charge of it. Walk, don't just stand there." I could feel real strength coming from Tommie, and I tried to apply it to myself.

More than anything else, I was grateful to Tommie for those lessons in *track feeling*. I learned how to be dedicated and involved in my own physical exertion. None of the women I had known in athletics had taken their sport this seriously. The women's attitude was always, "Do your best, but don't overstrain yourself." With Tommie I discov-

Executing the baton pass is one element of that glorious "track feeling" I learned to love at San Jose State.

CREDIT: Orin Collier

ered that I would survive no matter how hard I worked. I endured moments of intense pain during which I wondered whether I would ever draw a comfortable, nonhurting breath again.

At first, the physiological pain I felt in my workouts scared me. I was thrown out of equilibrium. My breathing was deeper than ever before and my heart pounded at a terrifying rate. That total, deep-down fatigue that expresses itself as a smothering blanket of pain throughout the entire body was brand-new to me. However, I was eventually going to become addicted to that feeling. It was the most satisfying part of the workout. The deeper you could push your body into that "beyondness," the deeper the pleasure that you would experience afterwards.

Over the years, I became familiar with that "out of equilibrium" feeling, and it no longer was frightening. No matter how totally winded you are, no matter how completely you gave of your energy in that last 330, no matter how drained you feel, you know that after a matter of minutes your body will regain its composure and be that much better for the effort.

After the workout you kicked back and took pride in the work your body had done. You could still feel the oxygen swirling through your bloodstream trying to replenish starving muscle cells that had given their all only several hours before. That "oxygen debt" that had accumulated was paid back in the postworkout hours, and that was the most pleasurable time. That was the time of the "natural high." Camaraderie among athletes reaches its peak during those hours because everyone is experiencing the same joy and pride in physical accomplishment. It is easy to feel close to people with whom you spend much time during that "high."

Those first few months I couldn't do a hard workout without Tommie, but later, as I began to build my own sense of self, I used the inspiration gained from him to further my own track goals.

Occasionally Bud called for a grand finale to the workout: "All right everyone . . . Killer-Dillers." Whenever we heard that, we knew we were in for real pain. Oddly, however, we didn't complain—I suppose because we knew that our performance wouldn't be judged by any external criteria. The exercise was a test of our own wills against our bodies. If our heads were right, we could always come out the winner. The extra conditioning and mental toughness we gained was invaluable.

Each of us started jogging around the quarter-mile track. Bud whistled and we began to sprint. That continued until Bud whistled again. Then we would drop back into a jog. We repeated that sequence eight or ten times until we rounded the final turn of the track. Then Bud produced a high-pitched series of whistles and started yelling, "All-away, all-a-way, all-a-way!" We knew we had to give whatever we had left in sprinting those last 60 to 80 yards to the finish. The run was a real killer, but a real satisfier, too.

I could tell when Tommie was pleased with his workout. Despite extreme fatigue, he'd summon enough energy to throw his arms in the air, throw in the appropriate dance steps and gestures, and act out his animated version of "Ain't Too Proud to Beg" by the Temptations, the number one soul song of the day. After a hard run together, I loved seeing Tommie so exuberant and alive; the closeness our shared workouts created made me fall completely in love.

6

A Patch of Blue, Huey Style

"Bigot!" I screamed and slammed the door.

"I don't care what you call me," my father yelled. "I don't want that man to ever set foot in this house!"

A visit home was no longer the happy occasion it used to be. Now, as I drove away, my father's threats rang in my ears. "I won't pay for any daughter of mine to go to college if all she's going to do is waste her time seeing a bunch of Negroes. You continue to see that man and I'll . . ."

Did Dad really say all that? I wondered if that narrow-minded man was really my father. My relationship with Tommie was forcing me to see my family, my friends, and my life in a whole new perspective. Lynda Huey, cheerleader and all-American girl, suddenly faced the realization that she did not live in Wonderland.

Those clever little racial jokes we made as teenagers

didn't seem so funny any more. I cringed as I remembered naming my old black Volkswagen the "coon cage," and going shopping at the "spic" market. "Ah loves you honey but youse the wrong culuh," we'd say for a quick laugh. Now the joke was on me.

That day I watched him run in Santa Barbara for the first time, I thought that Tommie was going to be different from anyone else I'd ever met. Such a big deal had always been made about "Negroes" and "whites" that I had assumed we wouldn't even speak the same language, let alone start spending time together. I guess I was curious and in awe of this man at first, but quickly I found that I simply enjoyed his company. I was growing fonder of him every day. But the repercussions I was facing because of him were also growing every day.

The myth of black sexuality was so strong it scared away white men who otherwise would have dated me. Apparently they feared that anything they had to do with me physically would be inadequate after I'd had a black boyfriend. The irony was that for a long time I didn't know a thing about sex, and no man respected my innocence more than Tommie.

Still, the gossip and the subtle rejections hurt, and no one offered me support. As I look back on that year, my naiveté astounds me. I was so proud of Tommie that it had never occurred to me that anyone would disapprove of our relationship. I thought dating Tommie Smith, world-record holder, would give me new, higher status. I was wrong. My friends thought that Tommie was seeking status by dating blond, white me. Sure, he was more talented than any of my previous boyfriends. Sure, he was good-looking, kind, a terrific dancer, and fun to be with. But Tommie was also black and therefore not a real person. The more I tried to make him real to my family and friends, the more they rejected me. In the end, I had to hide the relationship from my folks and keep justifying it to my friends.

My double life hit me hardest the summer afternoon that my sister Margie and I gave a surprise twenty-fifth anniversary party for my parents. More than fifty people came—relatives from all over the state and people from our church. The relatives I hadn't seen in years were doting on me while I looked around the room and tried to picture what would happen if Tommie suddenly appeared. He would have been greeted by gasps and incredulous stares, and all praise for me would have evaporated. I wanted him to appear; I wanted to expose all these people for what they were—bigots, like almost all the white people I knew. I had to struggle not to show open hostility to my relatives and friends. And I never went to church again.

The racism in my family and friends shocked me, but it came as no surprise to Tommie. He expected it and he knew how to defend himself. Tommie's defense mechanisms were working from the moment we met.

We talked the first day we met at the Santa Barbara relays, and by the end of the meet we were on our way to becoming friends. Bud Winter offered me a ride back to the UCSB campus on the team bus, and I gratefully accepted. Tommie and I strolled toward the bus, which was parked next to the beach.

I decided that the water looked too inviting to ignore and on an impulse jumped onto Tommie's back—to his surprise—and yelled, "Gimme a piggy-back ride." He was game, and off we went, laughing hysterically as we ended up rolling in the seaweed on the sand. Then we tried to determine who could walk on his hands the furthest. I won, so Tommie turned the game into a dance contest; and there he had me beat.

We saw the bus beginning to leave, so we ran to catch it. The instant we got on the bus the terrific feeling that had been flashing between Tommie and me stopped. I looked around for two seats so that we could sit together, but he motioned for me to sit somewhere else and quickly slid into the seat in front of me by himself. I wondered what that was all about until I realized how conscious Tommie was of the color barrier.

As our relationship developed, I was to be hurt again and again by Tommie's caution. I lived my life openly. I was proud of him, and I wanted him to be proud of me, yet often he would ignore me or deny any relationship with me to his friends. Sometimes I interpreted his discretion as a deliberate attempt to hurt my feelings.

Sometimes I worried that he was ashamed of me. When Tommie had to appear socially at a banquet or dance, he took a black date. In May of my sophomore year we ran in the San Jose State Invitational Track Meet and we both won our 100-yard dashes. Tommie virtually ignored me, destroying my visions of Nureyev and Fonteyn. I suppose he was afraid that our relationship would somehow become obvious to the 3000 people in the stands.

Gradually I came to understand Tommie's reasons for caution. The naive all-American cheerleader came to understand a shockingly different American experience. Tommie and his roomate, S. T. Saffold, the campus basketball star, told me tales of lynching, castrations, and killings of blacks in the South. At first I refused to believe their stories, so they pulled out the Encyclopedia of American Negro History to convince me. They seemed to know those books by heart and seemed to enjoy watching me cringe as they read to me the story of black suffering. At first I naively insisted that no one alive today would be capable of such prejudice; but as the people I knew began reacting violently against my relationship and the pressure to stop seeing Tommie continued, I came to see why Tommie never felt quite comfortable or safe. On the one hand, people idolized him as a sports superstar; on the other, he was less than human. The contradiction inevitably created tensions and hurt our relationship. He feared what could happen to him if he associated with a white woman.

Of course I never really escaped the prejudices of my own white environment. At the beginning of our relationship, I had misgivings. Sidney Poitier helped resolve my doubts in a movie called *A Patch of Blue*. The film showed a blind white girl falling in love with Poitier. Aha, instant justification for my relationship with Tommie.

My conviction grew as I recalled my family history. I remembered Mom telling the story of her own mother's guilty secret of the Indian blood in our family. Although my grandmother warned my mom that "they'll call you half-breed if they find out," my Mom never seemed ashamed of her Blackfoot blood, and as I grew up she gave me a special pride in my heritage. "That's why I'm so fast," I'd tell my friends. Tommie also was part Indian; his ancestry showed in his almost reddish complexion and high cheekbones. At one time when my mother was anxious about our relationship, she consulted a spiritualist. "Don't worry," the spiritualist told her. "This young man and woman were runners for the same tribe in their past lives. This relationship will lead to friendship and love. No marriage will occur."

If the spiritualist's theory helped Mom, I'm grateful. Only recently have I come to realize the anguish my relationship with Tommie caused her. At the time, I felt that my parents disapproved of our involvement solely because of prejudice. But recently Mom showed me a note she had written to herself during that troubled first year of my knowing Tommie:

A Christian nation we are supposed to be! What hypocrites! "We are all brothers and sisters in Christ," we teach our children. We love all races equally. Our children believe us and live their lives in brotherly love. Then something happens to this beautiful life we have seen flower into lovely womanhood. She sees no difference in color of skin; and becomes very attracted to a boy of the Negro race, and she is a mixture of Caucasian and Indian. The anger she feels to the "white" man for the way he treated the "red" man sends her even deeper into this relationship. Now she is very protective and defensive about seeing the boy and is blind at times that this could lead to marriage and the "HELL" that society puts mixed marriages through. This is my conflict and anguish: that the society she has loved and been a part of would crucify this lovely daughter of ours.

My mom was worried that I would be crushed by the rejection of people around me. She has since learned that I can withstand subtle and even overt racism. She has seen me stick by my black friends in uncomfortable moments and she knows now that I will continue to associate with friends of all persuasions. I was gratified when my parents came to visit me recently on a weekend when my house was hopping with track athletes on their way to a nearby meet. My parents seemed finally to enjoy meeting my black friends, rather than merely tolerating what they considered to be distasteful encounters in earlier days.

In those earlier days my folks were concerned that my friends, many of whom rapidly became ex-friends, disapproved of Tommie. Giving them the benefit of the doubt, I concluded that their prejudice was caused by a lack of exposure. Certainly, in 1966, my friends had almost no way to make black friends; racial segregation limited whites as much as blacks. Racial stereotypes were certainly alive and well on the San Jose campus. If you met somebody black on campus, you could safely ask him what sport he played. And SJS had only a handful of black women students, usually from prosperous black families who could afford a college education. (The Economic Opportunity Program, which began in September 1968 and was discontinued in 1974, did admit hundreds of minority students to SJS.) No wonder whites viewed blacks as creatures from another world.

I, too, had been ill at ease when first surrounded entirely by black company. But I also tuned in almost immediately. Black slang confused me at first—then captivated me. The blacks I met through Tommie had an animation and vitality that I had not encountered before. The men's track world was heavily black and, although my white friends criticized me, I was readily accepted in the black sporting life. Through Tommie I came to know other black athletes, and I learned about the track parties that took place after every important meet. All the athletes knew each other because they saw each other every week during track season as they traveled around the country. The tracksters stayed at the same hotel and promptly began tearing it up after the last race of the evening. After a meet in San Diego, in February 1967, I finally got to help tear.

Ralph Boston was impromptu host at my first track party. I quickly decided that Boston was the funniest man in the world. No one at the party had a record player, so the radio was tuned to Wolfman Jack coming in full blast from Tijuana. Ralph was trying to outhowl the Wolfman. Hands were clapping, fingers popping, and I loved that whole room swaying in time to dances like the Philly Dog and the Skate. I had struggled to learn to dance like Tommie, and that night I had my big debut.

"How come that gray chick can dance?" Boston asked after seeing me on the floor with Tommie and Lee Evans.

"She's from San Jose, ain't she?" they answered coolly. I felt that the world was mine that night, and I couldn't get enough of the party.

Comfortable moments like that were rare; other aspects of Tommie's black culture confused and upset me. I had not yet emerged completely from the conformist attitudes that had been ingrained in me in high school. Half of me was exhilarated by the new world I encountered; the other half still lived by Leigh High School rules of propriety.

I was a victim of that "how to win a teenage boy" philosophy. If I called him one time, Tommie had to call me back before I could call him again. If he didn't write me a letter when he was away at a track meet, then I couldn't call him on his return until he made an effort to see me. But Tommie didn't understand these high school niceties, and again and again we hurt each other as I tried to play a new game by old rules.

Tommie's insisting on secrecy caused more conflicts. Tommie didn't want us to be seen coming or going from his apartment together. He made me wait in the car until he was safely inside the apartment. Any public meeting was cause for rejoicing, an event to be noted in my diary:

June 11, 1966

TOM BROKE ANOTHER WORLD RECORD— the 220 curve. Henry Carr had the record at 20.2 and Tom did it in 20.0 and won the meet's outstanding athlete trophy.

After the meet I ate dinner with the team at the El Rancho Diner in Sacramento. That was the first time I was out in public with Tom. We rode back on the bus together, even though he was careful to sit apart on the way up.

I hated having to be quiet about having a superstar, a real international superstar, in my life. I wanted the world to know. But Tommie, by contrast, was a very private person and scorned what he considered my indiscretions.

Tommie and I developed an on-again, off-again relationship. He was torn between his black world and his affection for me. I was truly confused.

Although I was not active in the civil rights movement, my association with Tommie and his friends affected me in much the same way that participation in a black voter registration drive affected other women who were later to become feminists. For the first time I saw social injustice in America. My eyes were opened and I realized that America was not the land of opportunity I'd learned about in my Leigh High civics class. In 1966 I worried about injustice to blacks and calmly accepted the inferior sports program available to women at my own college. The way the world operated, women's second-class status seemed natural. Only later did I make for myself the same demands that I had made for my black friends. Only later did I realize that women, too, are entitled to the same equal opportunity and freedom from society's long-held prejudices.

7

→≫ ≪←

Separate and Unequal

If the color of our skins drove Tommie and me apart, our love of track was a bond between us. My track life took on a new importance thanks to my relationship with Tommie, and, of course, I was interested in his record-setting career.

Through Tommie I learned firsthand the pressures that face a superstar athlete. Take the nerve-shattering duel that Bud Winter staged between Tommie and Lee Evans, at that time the world's top quarter-miler. Tommie and Lee had been best friends until Bud predicted a new world record in the 440 at the San Jose Invitational and loaded the race with the fastest quarter-milers around in order to draw a capacity crowd.

That year Lee had not been beaten in the 440, and Tommie had not run an open quarter-mile—only 440 relay legs. The pressure hit them both hard. Monday Lee ran on one

Tommie Smith set a world record in the 440 when he broke the tape I'm holding at the San Jose Invitational meet in May 1967.

CREDIT: Sheedy and Long for Sports Illustrated

half of the track and Tommie worked out on the other. Neither one spoke to the other. On Tuesday, Tommie ran 352 yards in 33.2 seconds in a practice. (A 352-yard run might seem a strange distance, but Bud considered it the best prognosticator of a quarter-miler's potential time in a race without the athlete having to run a full exhausting 440. He added 10 seconds onto the 352 time, and the total gave him the 440 speed the runner was capable of that day. That meant that Tommie was capable of a 43.2 440 that day—world-record speed.)

The 440 hadn't been Tommie's race that year; he had been specializing in 220s and 100s. Lee knew that, but he also knew that Tommie had more natural speed. Lee hoped to win by showing greater endurance over the longer distance. Tommie's 33.2-second 352 started a lot of whispering that week and sent Tommie into a disappearing act until the weekend.

Saturday morning, before the race, Tommie and I rode

over to the track and carefully scrutinized lane 3 all the way around the cinder track. (San Jose State's tartan track wasn't built until the following year.) We wanted to be sure to remove any leaves or grit that might have been blown onto it—Tommie wasn't taking any chances. I could sense the tightness in his stomach, and I respected it with silence. But the moment the gun fired that afternoon I gave a loud "Go Tommie!" and yelled all the way to bring my hero home. I was as close as humanly possible to the tape—I was holding it. As they neared the finish line, I could see Lee's arms and legs churning frantically in lane 4. His head was rolling from side to side—a sure signal that he was giving everything he had for those last 100 yards. Tommie slid by Lee on the inside lane and hit the 400 meter tape in 44.5 and the 440 tape I was holding at 44.8—two new world records. Bud got what he wanted—a huge crowd and his world record. But unknowingly, I think, he created an animosity between Tommie and Lee that lasted quite a while. Because of his year-long performance, Lee was ranked the top quarter-miler in the world by *Track and Field News.* But Lee always knew that Tommie, a sprinter, had beaten him in a major race. Lee's right to the number one spot will always be a hot topic for debate in the track world, all because of that race, a race the two had secretly agreed never to run.

As I watched Tommie excel, my own track situation seemed more and more frustrating. Part of my problem was psychological; my erratic relationship with him drastically lowered my concentration on my athletic goals. All he had to do was appear at the track and he could destroy a good workout. If he wanted me to join him in something, I'd immediately stop whatever I was doing to be with him. If he chose not to speak to me that day, I would be miserable and unable to finish my workout with any real oomph. Time and again I made resolutions to take control, only to feel my willpower dissolve when Tommie walked into the room or onto the track.

I don't think I was particularly weak-minded. Love crises

and identity crises are not unknown among nineteen-year-olds. Most athletic programs for men are structured to give technical and important psychological support to young athletes. I had no solid ground on which to build my athletic career. The help Tommie gave was limited, because of the complicated nature of our relationship and because he had to think about his own workouts. Like Tommie and any other athlete, I needed regular, systematic coaching. Unlike him, I had to scramble for every bit of advice and help I could get.

For a long time my association with the men's team offered me my best opportunity for help. Don Geyer, an assistant coach at SJS, was the first to help me specifically with technique. Even before Bud began to include me in sprint-form drills, he saw that I didn't know a thing about sprint form, and he taught me the technique from the ground up. Don's informal coaching sessions were the first times that anyone had even suggested to me that I wasn't sprinting properly. I had a high back kick on my stride—an absolute waste of motion—and had no front knee lift at all. Don told me that I was probably losing a foot on every stride I took at top speed.

His help was invaluable, and his interest made all the difference in the world. When I worked out alone, I often quit early; but with Don around, I stayed to the end because I knew someone was interested and watching. What I needed even more than that was someone to give me steady leadership, someone to say, "Your next meet will be in two weeks. These are your weak points. This is what you'll do for workout to get ready for the meet. We'll see what your performance tells us and see what you need to alter in your workout as we go along."

Through Bud Winter and assistant coaches like Geyer, San Jose State gave exactly this sort of help to men. Yet, I had to watch the guys workout and try to pick up pointers. I had to decide which workout would be appropriate for a particular stage in my development. I even had to carry my own stopwatch if I wanted to time my 220 intervals.

The San Jose State women's track team was a well-meaning farce. As I said earlier, coach Carol Luther was a fine woman and a good athlete, but she didn't know much about track technique. The college officials obviously didn't care enough about women's athletics to supply funds to hire coaches who knew each specific sport. Although I ran with the women's team, I knew from the first practice that I was better off learning what I could from the men. At our first meet, the women on the San Jose team didn't know anything about how a track competition was organized. Every step had to be explained—heats, then qualifying rounds, then finals. My teammates had never heard of "high knees" or proper arm action. No one had told them how to hand off a baton in a relay or how to outlean an opponent at the finish of a tight race. Thanks to my natural speed and the bits of technical information I'd gathered from working out with the men, I easily outran my teammates. At college meets I could do everything wrong and still win. In fact, I was so bored at one meet that I actually stayed in the blocks a split second after the gun went off to give my opponents a head-start and myself a challenge.

SJS's main regional women's intercollegiate track meet was held at Humboldt State College, near the California–Oregon border. Many of the west coast colleges didn't have teams, so the competition was generally limited to eight or ten colleges in northern California and southern Oregon. In my freshman year, nine of us packed ourselves and our belongings into a station wagon. We didn't have uniforms so we brought T-shirts and shorts; I was the only one who had spikes. Eight crunched and cranky hours later we pulled into the Humboldt State gymnasium and set up camp. We assembled wrestling mats and sleeping bags for beds, and downed the bag lunches we brought for dinner —not what I would call optimum prerace preparation.

Somehow SJS pulled it off. I won all three of the sprints: the 50, 100 and 220. I still basked in whatever attention I could garner from my sports accomplishments. When the track announcer noticed me going through my high knee drill, he boomed across the loudspeaker, "And here ladies and gentlemen is San Jose State's female version of Tommie Smith." I delighted in the compliments and the smallest notice—an announcer praising my performance or a mention in a newspaper article was enough to get me going. Every time I ran at Humboldt I got the same supercharge of recognition, but I hated the morale-blasting amateurishness of the other participants. I remember my fury as the other competitors made comments like, "I really don't want to do this," at the starting line. Their hesitation, their giggling, and their clumsiness took away some of the legitimacy of the athletic contest and lowered my own view of myself as an athlete.

Lack of financial support for women's track was the key reason for the low level of competition. While athletic scholarships, high-paid coaches, and other kinds of material help were available for men, women's athletics went penniless. The story of the Tennessee State track team proves what a difference money makes. When I was in college, Tennessee State was one of the few colleges in the country to offer athletic scholarships to women in track. Not at all coincidentally, Tennessee State's TigerBelle team produced many of the top women track athletes, from the legendary Wilma Rudolph to Olympic gold-medal-winning sprinter Wyomia Tyus, to Martha Watson, Iris Davis, and Mamie Rallins—all veteran Olympic athletes.

In contrast to our paltry women's college meet at Humboldt State, Tommie's track season was filled with exciting competitions. Major relay meets were held all over California, and I envied my men track friends every time I sat in the stands at Modesto or Fresno and heard the starting gun. Each June the men packed their bags for the National

Collegiate Athletic Association Championship track meet and again I was struck by the excitement of their track careers compared to mine. But to use a contemporary phrase, my consciousness was far from raised. I was still enough of the cheerleader to enjoy rooting for men, and it hardly occurred to me that women should have important track meets. When I was in college there was no national collegiate track competition for women and, sad to say, I never even knew at the time how much I missed it. I was angry and accepting at the same time.

Women's college track at SJS was strictly amateur hour, but the AAU club system promised a higher level of competition. During my freshman year I worked out once a week with the Santa Clara Valley Girl's Track Club and ran in regular AAU meets every Saturday from March through June. Many of the AAU women were excellent athletes, and I enjoyed running against women who knew more than I did.

Then, just before my sophomore year, the Santa Clara team dissolved. I thought I'd simply go find a new team until I discovered an interesting twist to the AAU rules. According to the AAU, an athlete who wishes to change from one team to another must run on "unattached" status for a specific period, currently four months, but then one full year. If the Santa Clara team had completely folded, I would not have been bound by the waiting period. The AAU would have ruled that the Santa Clara athletes had no team and therefore were not held to the unattached rule, which is designed to keep athletes from hopping back and forth between teams. But the Santa Clara administrators had filed membership papers; the team still existed—if only on paper—and all of us ex-Santa Clara athletes were prevented from competing for any other team that year.

The loss of even the marginal support afforded by the AAU track team made my athletic life doubly difficult. Normally the team informed its athletes about meets and handled the entry forms. Now we had to scramble for information about meets. For workouts I was even more dependent on my association with the men's track team. And too often I worked out with the fellows to prepare for an AAU meet only to find that I had been given the wrong information about the time and place.

After a while the coaches of the Millbrae Lions track team in Millbrae, 40 miles north of San Jose, took pity on me. Ed Parker and Dr. Harmon Brown realized that I would eventually be free to join their team and did their best to keep me posted about track events. At times they even let me slide into meets with their team when I forgot to register in advance. The Millbrae Lions were a well-organized, well-coached team, and I was anxious to join it as soon as possible.

But good as Millbrae looked to me, I realized that it too had its problems compared to well-heeled men's college teams. The team was a community-sponsored effort; the coaches and doctor donated their time because they believed in women's track. The money for uniforms, travel, lodging, track shoes, and other track necessities had to be raised by the Millbrae Lions Club or through our own cookie sales, car washes, and paper drives. Many weekends that could have been better spent in training were devoted to earning money in nickel and dime operations. I could hardly picture Tommie Smith or the other San Jose superstars baking cupcakes to raise money for their track shoes.

Millbrae, although located too far away from San Jose to offer me the steady support I needed, proved to be a valuable experience. Assistant coach Dr. Harmon Brown, who has served as team physician for numerous U.S. track and field teams, was one of the most honest and fair coaches I've ever encountered. Concerned and mild-mannered, he knew how to deal with each individual athlete's weaknesses and strengths and was one of the few coaches who saw his athletes as whole people with lives outside the circle of the track. His concern and support helped me through several shaky time periods.

At Millbrae for the first time I made friends with women athletes who took their sport as seriously as I did. Ginger Smith from Stanford, hurdler and sprinter, was my competitor and friend, and for years we teamed up on winning relays for Millbrae on Saturday, then anchored relays against each other on intercollegiate meet days. Ginger was about my size, 5'4", 120 pounds, with bright blond hair and a super strong attitude. Whenever I doubted myself as an athlete and wondered whether I should concentrate on traditional feminine concerns instead of running around a track, I reminded myself that Ginger considered track important in her life, too, and Ginger's attractiveness and femininity were beyond question. She too trained with her school's men's team.

Although my conversation often centered on the male San Jose track heroes, Ginger kept her own goals and accomplishments firmly in view. She could never understand my choosing to watch Tommie run in a race instead of competing myself. She had a solid sense of herself, and she gave me the strength to continue competing when I was tempted to pack away my spikes and make life a lot easier for myself.

My outlook as an athlete was not improved by my rocky love life. All during my sophomore year, my relationship with Tommie waxed and waned. Tommie went abroad for track meets and brought loving letters and poems home to me. A month later another girl was wearing his sweater. Again and again I tried to get control of myself. I remember making a New Year's resolution on December 31, 1966, to begin a disciplined program to gain control of my mind, body, and spirit. That day I had run in an AAU meet and won two first places, but I hadn't felt as if I had done well at all. My times were second-rate, and I knew I could do better. I resolved to be in control of my life. If I could discipline myself to finish eight hard 220s during a workout when the pain got unbearable, I was sure that I could control my head the same way.

My self-discipline was never as strict as I hoped it would be, perhaps because the absence of a supportive environment made it difficult to look ahead and see real rewards for my efforts. But at least it was a turning inward. I was beginning to look to myself for strength. I also decided to broaden my friendships so that I would not be so exclusively dependent on my male track friends and specifically Tommie. Ginger was a woman friend for track; and Linda Vachon became my henchwoman in the social world.

I'd always dreamed of having a twin sister, a partner and a pal as energetic as myself to share my adventures. For a long time, Linda, my roommate and best buddy, came as close to that ideal as anyone could and was the instigator of some of my greatest good times. Linda is hard to describe because she is as changeable as a chameleon. When I met her she weighed 115 pounds; but she's weighed between 130 and 98 pounds. She has long blond hair one year, short dark blond hair the next, streaked medium hair a few months later, and then back to a natural brown. She loved to wear army jackets and loafers everywhere; then suddenly she would show up dressed straight out of the fashion magazines. She had a touch of royalty in her bearing one day, and was an imp the next.

Linda could start anything, walk up to anyone and get a conversation going. I loved to watch her in action. We were a mutual admiration society. I applauded her dramatic and singing triumphs; she took a proud interest in my track and field hockey achievements. We decided that we didn't always need men to make our lives important. Not that we decided to become nuns. Linda was a daredevil who liked men every bit as much as I did, but she didn't need a specific man to convince her that she existed. We took whirlwind weekend trips to Mexico, to Chico, Calif., to UCLA, and extricated ourselves from a hundred interesting tangles on fraternity row.

Sure we were rebels, but we definitely had a cause—ourselves. Tommie had opened my eyes to new perspectives on life, and Linda helped me see the possibilities of a new freedom from romantic domination. Linda made it a lot easier for me to deal with the day I found out that Tommie planned to marry Denise Pascal, a black track athlete whom he had seen often while dating me.

I remember meeting him the first time not long after the deed was done. Those same dark shades came toward me; I saw that long tall body I loved, the friendly smile. My heart leapt, then fell, as I listened to his friends congratulate him on his marriage. I realized at last that Tommie was out of my life for good. He had taken me far beyond my Leigh High School attitudes and introduced me to a far more complex and challenging world. I owed him a lot; to tell the truth, I still loved him a lot. But I knew an era in my life had ended—I had been hurt enough to grow up and I was on my own.

8

→》》 《《←

The Speed City Era

In the fall of 1967, San Jose, already known as a track and field stronghold, saw an influx of sprint talent that would soon earn it the name of "Speed City." *Track and Field News* gave the town its title after the world's fastest group of men were gathered there under the auspices of San Jose State and the nearby Santa Clara Youth Village Track Team (not to be confused with the Santa Clara Valley Girls' Track Club). Here was an all-star collection of speed that was dedicated to the principle that world track records were made to be broken.

Bud Winter had assembled the SJS speedsters, but the Santa Clara team, a dream relay, was largely the work of a super track fan named Art Simburg. Art, formerly the sports editor of the SJS college paper, the *Spartan Daily*, considered Tommie Smith the best thing to hit the track world since spikes but knew that Tommie's college eligibility was going to end and that he would be looking for an AAU club to represent. It had pained Art to see Tommie struggle as the anchor of the SJS teams when races had already been lost by second-rate runners ahead of him.

The idea of a dream relay team first popped into Art's head when he attended with Tommie the "Little Olympics," a pre-Olympic meet in Mexico City in 1967. When Art met Billy Gaines there and saw Gaines's incredible acceleration from the starting blocks, and learned that Gaines was interested in running for an AAU team, too, he saw a great possibility: if he could get Gaines and two other world-class sprinters, with Tommie as the anchor, he could put together a world-record-breaking team. Three months of high-pressure recruiting, hundreds of phone calls, and several Simburg-sponsored bus and plane trips later, Art had done just that. Now Tommie had a team worthy of his talents, and San Jose had the reputation as the fastest town in the West.

The dream relay team was impressive. Billy Gaines, a Mullica Hill, N.J., high school wonder, had already run 100 yards in 9.3 as only a junior. Billy had been unbeaten in the 60-yard dash during the previous year's indoor season and was considered by many track experts to have the fastest start. The second leg on the relay was to be run by Kirk Clayton, who had moved to San Jose from Grambling College in Louisiana. Kirk had lifetime best times of 9.3 in the 100 and 20.9 in the 220. After Kirk's performance in several Santa Clara Youth Village 440 relay teams, it became common knowledge that nobody could blow a race wide open on the second leg straightaway quite like Kirk. John Carlos, probably one of the most powerful men ever to run a relay turn, came third. "Da 'Los," as he called himself, had already run 9.2 and 20.3 lifetime bests while competing for East Texas State. Under Bud Winter's skilled guidance, the Harlem-born and -bred Carlos was sure to become one of the fastest sprinters in the world. And to anchor this dream team, Tommie Smith—the fastest relay anchor in the world.

The Santa Clara Youth Village team also included Jerry Williams, who often replaced Carlos as third runner in the relay. Jerry, a native Californian, had beaten Tommie in the 100-yard dash in high school, credentials good enough for membership in any gathering of super speedsters. But Art first had to convince Jerry to come off the block in Oakland and onto the track in San Jose. Jerry had been hustling for a living for over five years and hadn't run in that time. Martin McGrady heard about the gathering of speed in San Jose from his native Ohio, and decided to join. He was expected to dominate the middle distances in track while being Mr. Versatile. (Martin could compete in national competition in anything from a 110 to 880 relay leg and even ran the intermediate hurdles.) He would consistently beat the formidable Lee Evans in the 600-yard indoors.

This assemblage of stars formed unbeatable relay teams in major meets across the country. Ironically, the dream team of Gaines, Clayton, Carlos, and Smith never passed a baton around the 440 oval; these superstars were always too tied up with individual meet commitments to combine for the relay. On one weekend, for example, Gaines and McGrady were in the USSR, Smith and Evans were in Hawaii, Carlos was in Philadelphia, and Clayton and Williams were competing in southern California.

The talent on the SJS track, where the Santa Clara team practiced, was impressive, especially when added to the Bud Winter track team already there. The SJS relay team was only slightly slower with Frankie Slaton, Bob Griffin, Ronnie Ray Smith, Lee Evans, and Sam Davis to choose from. Every one of them had also run the 100 in 9.5 or better, so when the SJS and Santa Clara teams gathered for workouts, it seemed that bodies were literally

The Speed City Gang. Bottom row, from left: Tommie Smith, Ronnie Ray Smith, John Carlos; top row, from left: Kirk Clayton, Jerry Williams, Sam Davis, Billy Gaines, Lee Evans, Bob Griffin, Frankie Slaton.

CREDIT: Jeff Kroot

flying around the new SJS tartan track.

"What do you think of them?" Art asked me at the track one afternoon. For a while I didn't know what to think. The Speed City Gang caught me up in a whirlwind of excitement; all I could do was watch, listen, learn, and run like a madwoman to keep up.

Superstar sprinters tend to have appropriately dazzling personalities. They're cocky, clever, and as quick verbally as they are physically. Listening to that incredible bunch of men babble, at least three at a time as they warmed up, was an auditory trip in itself. You could hear a Louisiana accent coming from Kirk Clayton's direction, then the brisk New York–New Jersey interjections of Carlos and Gaines. A loud chuckle came from Tommie, a little Oakland street talk from Jerry, and then to top it all off, you'd hear Chris Papanicolaou, the Greek pole vaulter who was the first man to vault over 18 feet, yell "BOO-TEE-FUL!" as he stood in the pole vault pit and watched the guys sprint by in perfect form.

Each of these men thought he should be the star of the show and went to great lengths to attract attention. The east coast dudes were used to dealing with hats, so usually Gaines or Carlos appeared with the baddest "sky." When warm weather approached, Carlos decided he'd try something new and shaved his head. Jerry Williams usually came to practice in his classic gray sweats; Tommie appeared in his purple and green mismatches, singing "You Send Me" to anyone who would listen; Gaines and Carlos would come leaping over the fence in who knew what and McGrady made his entrance to the track walking on his hands and would end with a few backward rolls. No wonder this team picked up the nickname "The Flying Circus."

I loved the whole scene immediately. I warmed up with whoever happened to be jogging by when I arrived, then did my stretching exercises and calisthenics about 15 yards away from the omnipresent rap circle of energetic athletes. Palms were slappin' and words were flyin' as these dudes spent at least twenty minutes before workout each day just telling each other how *bad* they were.

Adrenalin flowed heavily on the track every day. With the 1968 Olympics only a year away, everyone was talking Mexico gold, and there was a real possibility that all of these runners could be on the USA team. And since everyone on the dream relay teams was either a sprinter or a quarter-miler, many of them were competing against each other for the same slots. Every day's workout became one more chance to psychologically whip the opponent. These men competed in the simplest training devices, and the easy warm-up drills before the workout often turned into all-out sprints between at least two of these crazy-men.

The fun often ran out of the dialog once the serious

workout began. No one seemed willing to give anyone else a word of encouragement or support. If anything, they seemed to do their best to destroy each other's confidence. At the same time, though, a family feeling grew among these San Jose superstars. Although each of these men was convinced that he was the fastest (to be the champions they were, they each *had* to believe that), tremendous respect flowed among them. If one of our superstars had to be beaten, he wanted to lose to a member of the family. Meanwhile they razzed each other along the way.

Jerry Williams and Carlos might be standing on the infield as Ronnie Ray Smith and Sam Davis came struggling off the turn, obviously out of gas. "Get them lazy knees up, Davis!" Williams would yell, then loudly proclaim to Carlos (his ally for this moment only), "There's two niggas we don't *never* got to worry 'bout."

"Yeah," Carlos would howl back. "My grandmother could kick both their asses and she only got one leg." Ten minutes later, words would be flying between Williams and Carlos. On this track it was every ego for itself.

Somehow I was the only female to fight my way into the midst of Speed City. And fight I often did. I was glad that I already felt at ease on my track before the new fast flock gathered there. Otherwise, they no doubt would have forced me to leave simply by making me feel uncomfortable.

"Get that little short girl off the track," John Carlos yelled one day, initiating a shouting contest in which my only major victory was my closing line, "If you ever shut your mouth, John, you'd lose half your face!" I jogged to the other side of the track and avoided John Carlos for the next year.

The men controlled the emotional climate at workouts. A few bad words from one of them ruined my workout that day. I couldn't concentrate on practice when my ego had just been deflated. That was one mentally tough bunch of men, and I had to learn to be just as tough or stay away. I fought back.

Bud Winter had always included me in the sprint form drills that took place every day, so that was at least a beginning. The guys would hear Bud specifically ask me to join the drill, so they had to assume that I must be something in the way of a legitimate athlete. One day Bud only had nine sprinters to work on relay passes, but needed ten to make up two relay teams of five each. He asked me to join. This drill had us in two's, spread out 110 yards apart around the track. The first two runners would sprint at three-quarters speed up to the next set of two runners who were waiting for them. They would pass the baton in good form to these two runners, then wait there until the baton had come back around to them. Then once again, they would take off, receive the baton, and run another 110 yards until all of us had done ten 110s. The men ran at half to three-quarters speed, but I had to race every single one of those 110s at an all-out pace just to stay even. I couldn't let my relay team fall behind. I nearly killed myself that day in practice, and in many practices to come.

I usually ran intervals with Ronnie Ray Smith, Bob Griffin, or Billy Gaines. In a typical Tuesday workout we ran five 220s with a 220-yard recovery walk between each one. The men gave me a 20- to 30-yard lead, then tried to catch me as soon as possible, while I tried to keep those footsteps behind me as long as I could. That way we all had to run hard. Gradually, grudgingly, these speedsters granted me a small amount of respect, and my own self-respect doubled as a result.

Gradually, too, Billy Gaines and I became good friends. I laughed the first time we met; he was only 5'8" and I thought he was so full of bullshit that I wondered how he stood up. But when we did starts together, he took time to explain to me why I should imitate him, rather than Tommie, who used a "tall sprinter's start." Billy had already figured out his own body and what it needed to stay in world-record condition. Now he passed on some of his knowledge, rituals, and exercises to me. He was the first person to make me believe that *I could be good*. He gave me incredible confidence simply by showing me what was necessary and how to do it.

Some afternoons we walked from the track to the football stadium and ran the slopes that arched up on both sides of the field behind the bleachers. I had never experienced such deep and total physiological pain in my life, but I found I was able to cope with it because Billy was so sure that I could. I started up the slope working on knee lift, good arm action, and rhythm. Billy let me get about 15 yards in front before he blasted up to me, then eased off. We finished the slope in perfect unison, Billy helping to pull me through those last 10 yards of straight-up-the-hill pain.

Usually, the sun was setting about the time we ran the slope for the third or fourth time, and the beauty of the sunset, coupled with the intensity of our shared physical experience, created an incredibly deep bond between us. A rush of pain hit me every time I reached the top of the slope, but the spirit moving next to me helped me fight that pain and an almost sacred feeling united Billy and me as we each threw an arm around the other on the way back down the hill to start all over again. I knew I could make it to the top each time because of the beauty that followed immediately after the pain.

But man does not run on beautiful moments alone— certainly not these superstars. Because they came from poor families who could provide no help with educational expenses, many of them were motivated almost solely by money, a motivation that never entered my athletic life because, as a woman, I couldn't expect material rewards. All the blood, sweat, and tears that I left on that track brought me not one watch, car payment, rent payment, scholarship check, or even one preregistration privilege. Fortunately my parents could afford to send me to school. These guys had to be money conscious, however, if they expected to survive financially. Their continual emphasis on making money for their talents was a necessity.

Discontent was rampant by the time Billy Gaines and John Carlos, last of the arrivals, appeared on the Speed City scene. The jobs that had been promised to each of the men hadn't turned up yet. Five of them were living with Art Simburg in a three-bedroom apartment. Countless inconveniences cropped up, threatening to make the dream relay team disappear almost as quickly as it had arrived. Billy promised to leave immediately if a job, a car, and a place to live didn't appear instantly; that had been part of the deal when he agreed to leave his comfortable life in New Jersey and come to San Jose. But nothing that had been promised by various club affiliates had been supplied. Martin, Kirk, Tommie, and Art wouldn't let the relay team fall apart only one week after it came together, so they scrounged enough money from their own pockets to pay a month's rent for Billy and to buy him what would soon become the notorious "yellow jacket," a faded yellow '58 Ford Fairlane that smoked so badly you could barely see the car. If we heard a roar and saw a cloud of smoke in the parking lot, we knew Billy had arrived. Billy had the nerve to put a "No Smoking" sign on the dashboard.

Jobs soon appeared. Woody Lynn, a coach of the Youth Village team, had some connections at Lockheed, so Jerry, Kirk, John, Martin, and Billy were soon employed there. They didn't seem to know what these jobs were, but they were getting paid, so they didn't much care. They told me that they were dusting doorknobs. Most of the guys didn't bother showing up at Lockheed after a few weeks. Who needed to sit doing nothing on a night job that lasted until I A.M. when you had to go to school the next morning and wear yourself out on the track all afternoon? The jobs at

Lockheed disappeared about as magically as they had appeared, and most of the guys had to hustle to keep their rents paid and their families in food. Many times I overheard phone conversations like this:

Track Star to Meet Director: "Uh, yeah, I *want* to run in your meet in Philadelphia, but the man in L.A. told me that he'll pay my rent this month. . . . Now man, you know I got a family . . . and you know they gotta eat. . . . Say what? Two plane tickets *and* my rent? . . . Well, yeah, maybe I *can* run this weekend in Philly. . . . When I get the tickets in the mail . . . no don't prepay them 'cuz I can't get those refunded. . . . Yeah, okay. . . . Thanks a lot man. . . . Yeah, you'll get your 6.0 all right. . . . I might get psyched up enough for a 5.9 if you make the money right. . . . Okay, man, see you next week."

The track star, who flew half-fare on his youth card, would have one and a half plane tickets to Philadelphia that he could turn into instant cash, and the meet manager could still say he had only provided transportation for an athlete and his wife to attend the meet. More money, in cash, was given when the athlete arrived at the meet. If Track Star didn't think the money was right, Meet Manager had to hold his breath throughout the performance and hope for the best. One track star was promised $600 to run the 600-yard dash, but was given only $500 upon his arrival at the track. Track Star led through the race until the 500-yard mark, then stopped and strolled off the track. As he said to Meet Manager, "You get what you pay for."

Many of these stars had trunk loads of Puma shoes that they auctioned off at school or used to raise a bid in a poker game. I couldn't believe it the first time I heard one of the guys yell, "I'll call that pair of cross-country shoes and raise you two pairs of spikes."

Where did the shoes come from? I learned one day when one of the men and I drove up to the Puma warehouse just south of San Francisco. From the way everyone greeted my companion, I knew he'd been there several times before. We walked through the front office into a gigantic warehouse full of athletic equipment, where half of the space was taken up with rows and rows of Puma shoes and the rest was filled with ski equipment. He headed straight toward the size 7s in the Puma section and started pulling shoe boxes off the shelves. He had five pairs of shoes under one arm before I realized what was happening. A travel bag or two thrown over each shoulder helped him carry the ski hats and windbreakers that he was gathering; a baton or two for good measure, two pairs of size 5 shoes for me, and we were out of there.

I was embarrassed that first time, but my companion's teasing had kept the warehouse staff laughing so hard they didn't seem to notice. If they did notice, perhaps they reasoned that the track fans, who were potential Puma shoes customers, would see what this superstar had on his feet as he crossed the finish line at a world record pace. In any case, the Puma people were used to seeing him in the warehouse and they soon got used to seeing me, too. I went back there several times within the next few months and became as bold as my friend by my second visit. If I saw something I wanted, I took it. I've never considered paying for a track shoe since.

9

→>> <<←

Seventeen Units of Life

Gradually the Speed City Gang came to dominate my life, in ways both good and bad. As an athlete, I learned a great deal from these superstars, fascinated as I was by their triumph, but by so doing diverted mental energy from my own fledgling efforts. As a friend, I had some real highs with these men, but I also had some of the most painful experiences of my life.

Perhaps the circumstances surrounding the San Francisco Cow Palace meet of the 1968 season illustrate the double-edged impact of the Speed City powerhouse. As the day of the meet approached, my stomach took a real beating. I felt I was part of the big time because the men I worked out with daily were the feature attractions, and I was one scared sprinter by the time Billy came over the night before the meet to psych me up.

I was leading off the sprint relay for the Millbrae Lions and had no experience starting on a wooden surface without starting blocks, so Billy was getting me ready. We put pieces of athletic tape down on the hardwood floors of my huge bedroom and I did practice starts at one end of the room, using the tape for traction, finishing with a dive onto the mattress we had put on the floor at the other end.

We knew that my main competition would come from Irene Obera of the Laurel Track Club in San Francisco, so Billy helped me run the race through in my mind five or six different ways to get my mind ready. In one mental race I led at the beginning; in another I had to catch her after the first turn; in another I caught her after the second turn —but I always imagined myself passing off the baton ahead of her at the end of my 160-yard lap. Billy wanted me to be mentally ready all through the race no matter what happened and to believe that I could be in front when the lap was over. How could I not believe Billy? He was so convinced I could do it that I knew I could too.

Excitement was high the day of that evening meet. There were the rituals: eating exactly five hours before race time, making sure the right spikes fit tightly in the right shoes. I tossed the baton around in my hand dozens of times to make it feel like a part of me. And just before meet time I lay still on my bed, listening to Donovan's "Season of the Witch."

But with my new friends at the meet, all my careful preparation went for nothing. My race was the next to the last event and I was too psyched up too early. I used all my adrenalin watching my men. The men's 60-yard dash ended with everyone on the floor because of a mishap with the rope that was supposed to help stop the runners at the end of the dash runway. After running full speed through the tape, runners have only about 30 feet to slow down before they meet the glass doors on the end wall. A thick rope is held up just beyond the finish line to give the sprinters something to grab and help them stop.

The rope men weren't on their job that night in San Francisco and had the rope practically on the ground as Billy Gaines and Charlie Greene tried to outlean each other across the finish line. As the runners reached down to grab the rope, the attendants saw that the rope wasn't in place and straightened it up to chest height. It hit Gaines and Greene in the throat, upended them, and sent them flying at full speed. Kirk Clayton tripped over the rope, hit the glass doors and wound up in the hospital with a concussion. O. J. Simpson, thanks to his football sure-footedness and the fact that he finished last and had time to see what was happening, was the only competitor on his feet at the end of the race.

The tension and drama left me wilted. By the time my race dragged around two hours later, I was limp. The gun starting my relay went off, but I didn't respond well. I ran, but I didn't sprint. I was in fourth place coming out of the first turn. Suddenly I realized that I had better start sprinting. I ran hard down the first straightaway and moved into second place. I tried to move past Irene Obera on the inside and felt her left elbow hit my shoulder. (That kind of physical contact is normal in indoor track, but I wasn't yet tough enough to retaliate.) I lost my balance and stepped onto the cement infield, slipped, then stepped back onto the track and fought her almost step for step down the last straightaway. Irene and I got in each other's way as we were trying to hand off the batons and chaos developed as it so often does in those tight indoor quarters. I ran past my teammate and had to turn around to give the baton to her behind me. Because of that bad hand-off we were back in fourth place again and we stayed there throughout the rest of the race. Surprisingly, I wasn't heartbroken over my performance. My own athletic encounter hadn't seemed important by comparison with the drama of the men's events.

No one seemed to notice my event anyway. Everyone

was still concerned about the sprinters who had been injured in the 60-yard dash, and I was concerned about what I had seen on the sidelines as photographers were running in to get pictures. A pregnant woman—the same one I had seen Billy Gaines with his first day in San Jose—was screaming frantically to him. I had assumed that she was his wife when I saw her with him that first day, but he had denied it. I had believed his story that this woman was not his wife, until a *Sports Illustrated* article came out that week describing the fall, the injuries, and the pregnant wife on the sidelines.

His wife's appearance should have ended my growing friendship with Billy. But even though Billy was a married man, I still cared very much for him. Obviously, the rules I had learned in childhood didn't fare well under the onslaught of real emotions.

I also saw Tommie often enough to remind me of his presence, and now and then I found myself still longing for his attention. Two married men were the men I most enjoyed being with. I couldn't believe how low I had "let my morals slip," and it hurt to think of my relationships in that way. I knew by thinking that way I was violating society's moral code, but my feelings didn't seem wrong to me.

My troubles concerning Billy Gaines weren't the only blow to my battered reputation. Most of my running buddies came to the Homestead (as the house I lived in came to be called) to rap, clown, and play after practice, and our carryings-on soon had the roommates, the neighbors, and just about all of the SJS campus ready to call the morals squad. I attributed a large part of their outrage to the fact that my buddies were black; if I'd had a circle of white friends doing the same kinds of things, I would have been considered a popular coed.

A rift soon appeared in our household; my roommates were divided into those who were willing to talk to all the black athletes and those who ignored them and went upstairs as soon as they appeared. Linda Vachon, who had become my best girlfriend, moved out of the room we shared and joined forces with those roommates who fought my growing involvement with black friends. Linda had accepted Tommie readily, since he was only one black and a star athlete. But when a lot of black tracksters started hanging around she turned her back on me. In losing Linda's friendship, I gave up a person who came closest to being a twin sister. The hurt was overwhelming.

Linda moved into another room at the Homestead and Lynn Gates moved into the room with me. We had been in several classes together as p.e. majors, but had not gotten to know each other until she came out for track. Once Lynn joined in my workouts, she could easily understand my involvement with these track men. While other men on campus were giving us the "oh, you're a jock" treatment, our track comrades were making us feel special and attractive.

Some friends pressured me to end my black friendships because as they put it, "you don't belong." The dissonance between the fun times I had with my black friends and the reprimands, advice, and warnings I received from my white friends left me more than a little confused. And then the rumors started. Since so many black men came to our house, I guess the lies were inevitable. A non-track observer couldn't know the interchange of strength and pain my athlete friends and I had known in workouts and couldn't understand the real basis of our friendship. It was inevitable that some people would conclude that my attraction for these men was purely physical. My roommates scorned me still further when the "Huey and her friends" stories started.

The stories hurt me, but even more so when I learned that several of the sprinters were actually claiming sexual conquests that had never occurred. I couldn't believe that the friendship I shared with these men had been so hideously distorted in people's minds. My life started to fall apart. I couldn't concentrate on school. I rationalized my absence from classes. I wasn't taking seventeen units of class that semester. I was taking seventeen units of life, and learning more than I had planned.

10

❧❧❧

Black Changes, White Reactions

I went through a tremendous upheaval during those Speed City years, but soon my black friends were to make greater and more significant changes in *their* lifestyles and attitudes. About this time, 1967–1968, the civil rights movement hit sport with a vengeance, and "Negro" athletes suddenly became "black" athletes. The change was evident in small and large ways. Blacks stopped apologizing for not being white. They refused to masquerade anymore, and the Afro hair style appeared on the black fashion scene as a symbol of black pride. They stopped believing in the whitewashed mass media and textbooks and demanded laws that protected their right to equality in this country. But most important, they insisted that white society treat them as human beings.

The average sports fan couldn't understand why blacks

used athletics as a vehicle for political change. Fans believed that sports had been good to the Negro. In the popular myth, athletic achievement offered black youngsters a way out of the ghetto and into a college education they couldn't otherwise afford. Certainly sports was one of the few arenas in which blacks could get wide recognition for their accomplishments, or so the fans thought.

The sham of racial equality in athletics hadn't yet been exposed to white America. But many black athletes knew that racism was as rampant as before, even though they themselves were being used as examples of democracy and equality. They knew that the percentage of black kids that made it out of the ghetto via athletics was so small as to be insignificant. They also knew that coaches used racial generalizations for determining athletes' positions in football and in track and field events. A young black track athlete would always be guided toward the sprints, hurdles, or jumping events, never distance or technique events that took "real perseverance or intellect." Black football players could count on running with the ball or catching it, but never throwing it themselves. Quarterbacking, too, required more brains and leadership ability than blacks had —everyone knew that.

So blacks competed for a few slots on a team, while the other positions were left open for white athletes. Most coaches kept to a minimum the number of black athletes who appeared on the field at any one time. This was a standard practice, one the coaches might not necessarily agree with, but that most alumni associations required. After all, how could the alumni possibly raise money for the school if there were more black kids out on the field than white? Nobody would contribute to a team like that, even if it was winning.

The black athlete looked at his world of sport and saw that it needed change. And he saw that through sport he might be able to change American society, even if only a tiny part of it. Prominence in sport gave blacks a weapon, and naturally they used whatever was available in their war against racism. Moreover, many top black athletes were concerned that they might be co-opted by white society. They were tokens who "proved" that the American dream was not an illusion for blacks. Many top black stars were unwilling to continue to be used as evidence in support of a lie.

Many earlier generations of black athletes had felt that they could best help themselves and their race by behaving politely and excelling in sports. At one point, humility and excellence probably did foster racial harmony, but now it was time for the black cause to move along. No longer was it enough for a black athlete to go to a college and run and jump and play ball for four years (and usually end up without a degree because coaches had shoved them through "Mickey Mouse" courses just to keep them eligible). Now blacks were demanding fair treatment all the time, not just when they were scoring points for their school. Blacks asked for what should have been theirs all along: a chance to live in an apartment close to school like all other students, a fair chance to earn a degree, and most important, respect as equal human beings at all times. That list seems reasonable enough, but in those days it sounded like a dream to most blacks. Fortunately there were big dreamers at San Jose State who made a historic innovation in the use of sport and the black athlete as leverage against a racist system.

Harry Edwards, sociology professor at SJS, had been a superstar on the basketball court in college, and at 6'8", 225 pounds, had looked so tough and so mean that two pro football teams had drafted him right off the basketball court. He also held the SJS school record in the discus for many years. Edwards is a giant physically and intellectually. He has charisma and cannot be intimidated. His size, intelligence, and forceful personality gain Harry the power to control things, to change things, and he knew a lot needed to be changed. He decided to start with the San Jose campus.

As soon as school opened in the fall of 1967, Harry organized all of the black students on campus (almost all of the seventy-two black students were male athletes on scholarship) and created the United Black Students for Action (UBSA). The first day of school they held a rally on 7th Street, the main forum for all student happenings. Their strategy was simple. They recognized, as others did not, that the athletic program at San Jose State was racist. They decided to use whatever leverage they could to pressure the college community to reform. Too often blacks had protested discriminatory treatment using an issue that was of limited concern to the people who were in positions to effect change. This time they decided to use something that was a central focus for the entire community—athletics. What could possibly be more important to a student body than its first football game of the season? The administration was concerned because of a possible breach-of-contract clause with the opposing school. The faculty of the men's physical education and athletics department were deeply disturbed.

Harry and his assistants wrote a list of demands that they presented at a rally. They stated there that the game would be canceled until the demands were met. Basically the demands were

Public deliberation of all problems faced by minority students at SJS.

Public announcements from SJS administrators that housing—approved, unapproved, fraternity, and sorority—that was not open to all SJS students would not be open to any SJS students.

Any student who insisted on living in segregated housing would be suspended from school until he conformed to the moral and ethical code of the college. This would also apply to all sororities and fraternities.

All social and political organizations on campus would be required to stipulate in writing that their organization was open to all SJS students. Those that did not would be disassociated from the college.

Equal treatment for all athletes by the athletic department.

A statement from the athletic department denouncing the racist fraternity system.

Use of the 2 percent rule to bring minority students to the SJS campus in at least the same proportion as their representation in the general population in California.

Harry and his crew were a fearsome sight standing in the middle of 7th Street with their signs and producing violent verbal outbursts. The group promised violence if the game was not canceled.

To the average white student on campus who was totally ignorant of black problems, the protest was quite a shock. "They never complained about anything before," whites said. "What's causing all of this anger all of a sudden?" Most of these students didn't realize that every one of the UBSA members had already suffered twenty-some years of daily abuse to rouse their anger.

The football game was canceled by San Jose's progressive president, Dr. Robert Clark. Almost everyone was relieved; a notable exception was an irate Governor Ronald Reagan, who publicly condemned both Harry and Dr. Clark. Reagan insisted that black students should not be allowed to coerce college administrators.

The UBSA had won, and eventually all of their demands were met. But more important, blacks had learned to use power. The black athlete and his UBSA supporters had found that they could exploit the white man's economic and almost religious involvement in athletics. The snowball started rolling in San Jose, but within the next few years numerous black athletes at campuses all over the country presented similar demands to their institutions.

During this period black attitudes changed radically. The most notable physical difference was the emergence of the Afro, or natural, hairstyle. One by one, my men friends started letting their hair grow to new lengths, proudly showing the world that they would emulate whitey no more. The women slowly started cutting their long, pressed hair and allowing its natural curliness to show. In those early months, a new Afro almost always meant that a black militant had been born. When a black woman started wearing a natural, you could count on almost open hostility if you were a white woman.

This was a difficult period for me. My closest buddies were black friends from the track. I could now feel a real ambivalence in our relationships. On the track, we shared the exhaustion, the excitment, and the exhilaration of the workouts, but when I ran into them on campus, they greeted me with a furtive nod or wave behind the back, and kept on moving. We no longer could be friends in public. Their new attitude hurt me deeply. I found it hard to laugh and play with people during half the day and then see them refuse to acknowledge my friendship during the other half. I had to keep reminding myself that most of them had lived their entire lives dealing with hypocritical whites and had suffered through similar experiences. That reasoning didn't ease the hurt much, however.

Harry Edwards remained a major figure in the UBSA, and he also became the local guru of the black movement. He taught a sociology class called Racial Minorities that during the 1967–1968 academic year grew from 30 students to more than 900. Harry created a black awareness on campus, and the more politically active and thoughtful white students were eager to understand the demands of blacks and how they planned to move toward their goals.

Harry was a master in public. He knew that his appearance could be overwhelming so he used that to advantage. The auditorium in which his class was held would be filled by class time. The crowd was usually fairly quiet except for some blacks who knew they had the whites at a disadvantage. They made racial jokes of their own; probably it was the first time in their lives they felt safe doing that surrounded by whites. Sometime before 7:15 (the class began at 7 P.M.) you could hear a rumble of whispers start at the back of the room and gradually build until a big, mean-looking black dude came strolling slowly down the middle aisle. Harry usually wore a black beret, an army jacket (with matches visible in the pocket), tight, tight pants, and big black glasses that accented his angry, fiery eyes. I loved it. I kept saying to myself "scare me, Harry, scare me!" By the time Harry reached the podium on stage, the white 60 percent of his audience was frightened, and the remaining blacks were giddy with pride. The blacks loved Harry and everything he had to say about the cracker, the honky. What a delight to them it was to hear him booming out insults at whitey and to hear black anger expressed out loud.

After three hours of listening to Harry, I walked out emotionally exhausted. Harry created a separatist doctrine that lumped me in the same category with all whites. I believed there could be a middle ground where blacks and whites could communicate. Harry described the white woman as a devil tempting black men. I wanted to stand up and scream that I had no devilish intentions on black men. These men were my friends. But who would have believed me? I knew Harry wouldn't; he was such a strong, forceful man that every time I was in his presence, I wasn't even sure I believed myself. Many times during this period my confusion became so great that I figured that the only way out of my identity crisis would be to wake up black one morning. Then I could join the black struggle for real. But that, obviously, was no solution. I was going to have to wrestle with this black–white issue on my own and eventually hope to reconcile it for at least one person—me.

11

⇢⟫ ⟪⇠

The Olympic Boycott Movement

Harry Edwards's lectures and example harnessed the energies of many of San Jose State's leading black athletes, and none of his political proteges became more controversial than the world-famous Tommie Smith. Tommie's extra notoriety began in the fall of 1967 when an enterprising reporter in Tokyo asked if there was any chance that the black athletes might decide to boycott the 1968 Olympic Games in Mexico City. "There's a possibility," Tommie answered, adding that the purpose of any boycott would be to protest racial injustice in America. At that point no boycott had been planned, but the wire services picked up Tommie's rather casual remark and blew it out of proportion, intimating that there was a strong possibility of an Olympic boycott. Tommie learned how fast the word had spread when he arrived in San Francisco and saw the airport swarming with television cameras and reporters. He wondered who the celebrity could be; then he found out: the man of the hour was Tommie Smith.

As the hate mail and death threats started to pour in from cranks around the country, Tommie and Harry decided to contact as many black athletes as possible to see how many would favor a boycott. After speaking with athletes from the local Bay Area and Los Angeles, Harry and Tommie felt they had enough positive reaction to call for a meeting of top black athletes from the entire country. In October 1967 the Olympic Project for Human Rights was formed.

On Thanksgiving weekend an Olympic boycott workshop was held in Los Angeles. Tommie, Lee Evans, Otis Burrell, and Kareem Abdul-Jabbar were the most prominent men in attendance, although many lesser-known black athletes from many states also came. Harry, Tommie, Lee, and Kareem voiced their support for the boycott movement. Several older athletes voiced objections to the plan, but were booed into silence. The meeting concluded with all but three of those present voting for a boycott. (The three opposing voters were not athletes.)

Most of white America, including me, found it difficult to understand the commitment of these black superstars. We saw the glamorous lifestyles of a handful of superstars, were ignorant of the living conditions of most blacks, and had to wonder what the superstars were complaining about. These athletes had the insight, though, to realize that if they hadn't been outstanding basketball players, or 27-foot longjumpers, or 9.1 sprinters, they, too, would be faceless black men trapped by racial discrimination. They had the social awareness to realize that the struggle of blacks in Fillmore, Watts, and Harlem was their struggle also. These black superstars were the few blacks in the country who had any wholesale ammunition for the fight against racial injustice. They had to use it. As Harry said, "We are putting Washington and the world on notice that

Harry Edwards (left) at a New York press conference in early 1968 talks about the planned boycotts of the New York Athletic Club Track Meet and the Olympics.

CREDIT: The New York Times

they can no longer count on the successors of Jesse Owens, Rafer Johnson, and Bob Hayes to join in a fun-and-games fête propagandized as the epitome of equal rights, so long as we are refused these rights in white society."

The first test of the strength of the boycott movement came in February 1968 when the New York Athletic Club (NYAC) held its indoor track meet at the new Madison Square Garden. All year long, NYAC, one of the few athletic facilities in downtown Manhattan, had closed its doors to blacks and excluded all but a few token Jews. But when the club sponsored a track meet and was looking for gate receipts, it sought out black superstar athletes to high-light its program with world-class talent.

The supporters of the Olympic Project for Human Rights felt it was time to regain some of the dignity black athletes had compromised over several decades when they participated in a meet run by a club that would not nor-mally allow a black person to shower in its facilities. The organizers contacted as many black athletes throughout the country as they could and urged them to bypass this track meet. Then they attempted to attract international atten-tion to their protest by sending a telegram to the Russian Embassy in Washington, explaining that the NYAC track meet would be picketed by black people protesting the racist exploitation of Afro-Americans by the sporting es-tablishment. The Soviet international touring team was in the United States competing in a series of indoor meets and planned to participate in the NYAC competition. The team was warned that their safety could not be guaranteed if they tried to cross the picket line, and was urged to support the black struggle.

The boycott of NYAC on February 15, 1968 was success-ful. All of the U.S. military teams were pulled out of the meet, the high school segment of the meet had to be can-celed due to lack of athletes, and many white and black colleges that usually participated in the track meet did not attend. At the last minute the Russian international tour-ing team also decided against participation. A show of black solidarity had been achieved. This boycott marked the end of an age in which black athletes would compro-mise their dignity for a radio, a television set, a watch, or even the simple love of competition. The next step was to unite with even greater strength for the Summer Olympics in Mexico City.

During the spring and summer of 1968, the Olympic Project for Human Rights remained prominent in the media. Hubert Humphrey, then vice president, criticized the boycott attempt at several news conferences. Articles about Harry and his project appeared in most of the country's major magazines and newspapers. And ironically, Avery Brundage, staunch defender of the apolitical tradition of the Olympic Games, inadvertently created much support for the boycott.

Brundage, president of the International Olympic Committee (IOC), organized support to have South Africa admitted to the 1968 games. South Africa had been banned from competition in 1964 because of its apartheid policies, and its readmission in 1968 led thirty-two African countries, as well as Cuba, Malaysia, India, Saudi Arabia, Iraq, Syria, Trinidad, and several Scandinavian and South American countries, to withdraw or threaten to withdraw from the games. In addition, the Soviet Union threatened to withdraw if South Africa was not again banned from the games—a move that would no doubt result in the departure of the entire Eastern bloc. The Soviet threat had to be taken seriously because two years earlier Russia pulled its team out of dual meets scheduled in Berkeley and Los Angeles because of American political and military involvement in Vietnam.

South Africa's admission to the games enhanced the clout of the American boycott. African and Afro-American athletes felt a real bond in their struggles to overcome a white oppressor. With the Ethiopian and Kenyan black stars out of the games, and with the American boycott gaining power each day, it was conceivable that not a single black athlete would show in Mexico City. Harry laughingly talked about the 1968 Summer Olympics as an all-white affair restricted to the United States and her satellite countries.

The Mexicans had already invested over $100 million in preparing for the games and were panicked by the prospect of financial disaster if the boycott was successful. High-ranking Mexican officials put intense pressure on Brundage, and he was forced to call a special meeting of the IOC executive board. Eventually South Africa was thrown out of the Olympics, and Harry Edwards commented to the press, "The exclusion marked a victory of international significance for the Olympic Committee for Human Rights and the Afro-American athletes whom it represented. For the first time Afro-Americans had united with other black nations to defeat forces in the world that were seeking to perpetuate racism and discrimination."

On April 4, 1968, America's foremost nonviolent black leader was killed. After the announcement of Martin Luther King's death, several of the Speed City Gang stopped by my house. I felt a real coldness and deep down anger in them that I had never seen before. Some of those emotions no doubt strengthened the attempt to make the Olympic boycott work. Demonstrations intended as solemn memorials to the late Dr. King were organized at the West Coast Relays, the California Relays, and the Olympic Trials held in Los Angeles.

Ordinarily these track meets were primarily black fashion shows and parties. But this time the party would have a little extra heat. All the brothers and sisters from Oakland, East Palo Alto, the Fillmore, south central Los Angeles, and Watts were on hand at the California Relays to lend their support to the black athletes on the track. And they wanted their presence to be felt by the white sporting establishment: black arm bands were worn by nearly every black spectator, Olympic boycott posters and Olympic Project for Human Rights buttons were visible everywhere, and huge sections of the stands became unified verbal machines supporting their black brothers on the track and filling both the athletes and themselves with pride. And whitey was scared; this obvious show of black solidarity surprised most whites in the sports establishment. Friends who I ordinarily would have sat with at the meets were in the thick of those black rooting sections, and I knew better than to try to speak with them as I walked quickly past the area to get to another section of the stands. My main hope was that no one would recognize me as I walked past because I didn't relish the idea of being taunted.

Each meet became a black–white competition. Whenever a brother crossed the finish line first, the black sections of the crowd would go nuts. Bongos and congas were played, and there was literally dancing in the aisles. The white members of the crowd couldn't ignore the fact that many, many events were won by black athletes. The sprints and the jumps were dominated by blacks; it was a rare white athlete who even made it to the finals in a 100-yard dash or the long jump. White America now saw very clearly just how much athletic strength would be lost if the Afro-American athletes decided to bypass the Olympic Games. Our world-record holders in every sprint event were black. America had two of the best long jumpers in the world—both black. The three best hurdlers in the country and probably the world also were black.

The men's Olympic Trials took place at the end of June in the Los Angeles Coliseum. Again, the stands were filled with black supporters, music, congas, and celebration. A meeting had been held in Los Angeles before the trials to unify the black athletes. Of twenty-six black athletes who seemed sure to make the team, only thirteen said they would definitely boycott the games. But if half of the athletes boycotted and the other half went to the games, nothing would be gained. Moreover, some black athletes—Jim Hines, for example—stated that they would go to the games no matter what. These men would replace such people as Tommie Smith or John Carlos and the boycotters' sacrifice would go unnoticed. Such a split would also threaten the growing unity of black athletes of all countries. The Olympic Project for Human Rights devised an alternative plan. Blacks would run in Mexico City, but each athlete would "do his own thing" on the victory stand according to his own dictates of conscience.

When the Olympic Games began, coaches of the track team and members of the U.S. Olympic Committee (USOC) pressured black athletes not to make visible protests on the victory stand. At first it appeared that the establishment had won. Jim Hines and Charlie Greene took first and third respectively in the 100 meters and were the first black athletes to take part in victory ceremonies. In San Jose we watched the ceremonies on TV in Ronnie Ray Smith's apartment. We didn't see a single sign of protest, and the mood of the blacks watching was angry. But then the black protest finally came to life when Tommie Smith and John Carlos won the gold and bronze medals respectively in the 200 meters.

Tommie took the stand wearing black socks, a black scarf around his neck, and a black glove on his right fist. John wore a black glove on his left hand. As the national anthem was played, they both bowed their heads and raised their gloved fists. Later, in an interview with Howard Cosell, Tommie quietly but carefully explained that the socks he wore symbolized poverty in black America. The scarf stood for black pride. The black fists represented black power and the arch created between the two fists stood for black unity. I watched the interview and took great pride in Tommie's courage. I knew him well enough to be sure he always did what he thought was necessary or right. I sent him this telegram: "Congratulations. You were beautiful . . . the race and interview. Such a beautiful example of black dignity." Apparently I was one of the few white people who felt that way about his actions. I was amazed at the animosity toward him.

"Sure, I sympathize with the problems of Negroes in this country," one white liberal said, "but what does that have to do with the Olympics? I'd give my right arm to have won a gold medal in the Olympics. Mexico just wasn't the right place to do something like that."

But where *was* the right place? When were blacks given such mass media attention? Perhaps these people were reacting to the newspaper and television reports that claimed that Tommie and John had been whistled and booed out of the stadium. Recently, however, I listened to a tape recording of the 200-meter victory ceremonies. Applause and gigantic sounds of approval welled up from the crowd. From what I heard on that tape the majority of the Olympic observers admired the black protest.

The USOC ordered Tommie and John out of Mexico within forty-eight hours and suspended them from the U.S. team. The committee also warned other American athletes that they faced severe penalties for any further black power demonstrations. But the USOC action backfired and created an avalanche of support among Olympians from all over the world. The Cuban men's 440 relay team dedicated their silver medals to Tommie and John. Countless African countries issued statements of approval commending the two men; the German 1600 meter relay team supported the demonstration, and Peter Norman, the Australian sprinter who had placed second in the 200-meter race behind Tommie, had mounted the victory stand wearing an Olympic Project for Human Rights button, an act for which he was heavily criticized by his own government. Tommie and John were heroes in much of the Olympic Village, in fact, in most of the world.

The United States chose to try to shame these men by sending them home and releasing stories to the media that portrayed them as villains. The United States, along with much of the rest of the world, had cheered the Czechoslovakian Olympic team and its individual members who publicly protested the invasion of Prague by the Russians; most of the world viewed the black power salute in much the same way. The mistreatment of blacks in America had been exposed at a world forum, and the world had applauded that exposure. Naturally, the white power structure of the United States was not pleased.

Black athletes who might well have steered clear of politics that Olympic year suddenly became protesters. Bob Beamon and Ralph Boston were two athletes who had hung back when the boycott originally had been discussed. However, they were so infuriated by the USOC action against Tommie and John that they mounted the victory stand (after winning gold and bronze medals respectively in the long jump) wearing long black socks in protest.

Then came the 400-meter ceremonies. The United States swept the race: Lee Evans won the gold, Larry James took the silver, and Ron Freeman the bronze medal. The three of them took the stand, waving and smiling and showing no sign of protest. We in San Jose were slightly disappointed because Tommie and John had taken such a strong stand. But, we rationalized, Lee wanted to run in the upcoming 1600-meter relay and was taking no chance of being kicked out of the games before then.

The U.S. 1600-meter relay team won their race and then approached the victory stand wearing black berets. They clenched their fists and good-naturedly gave the black power salute to the black section of the crowd. But because they stood at attention during the playing of the national anthem, the press and TV ignored their action and claimed there had been no protest. Although Lee and company did as much as Bob Beamon and Ralph Boston, black San Joseans thought Lee had failed them. When the three Olympians returned to San Jose, the black community gave Tommie and John heroes' welcomes; Lee was exiled from the San Jose black community for some time.

Dr. Clark, president of San Jose State, made it public knowledge that as far as he was concerned, Tommie and John "would not be received as outcasts in America, but as honorable men." Governor Reagan again censured the SJS president for his comments. The majority of students seemed to be proud of Dr. Clark's stand, even if they hadn't totally agreed with Tommie's and John's actions. Dr. Clark scheduled a welcome home ceremony on 7th Street the day they returned from Mexico.

When I finally got to spend some time with Tommie several days later, I asked all those questions that were bothering me. At that time Tommie hadn't had much chance to think about what happened, but since then he has told me more about his thoughts at the time of the demonstration.

I asked Tommie if he knew what John was doing behind him. "You know," he said, "no one's ever asked me that one. No, I had no idea what John might have been up to. He asked for one of my gloves when he saw what I was going to do, so I gave him one and said, 'Just do what I do.'"

Tommie told me that when he stood totally unprotected on the victory stand for those slow, slow minutes of the national anthem, he realized that he might be taking his life in his hands. I thought he was being a little melodramatic, but he said he had been threatened while he was organizing the boycott and that a boycott opponent had killed Harry Edwards's dogs and left them chopped up in pieces on Harry's front porch. And just a week before the 1968 Olympic Games began, the Mexican government had stopped a peaceful protest by Mexican workers and students with machine guns. These events prior to the Olympics made the possibility of death very real in Tommie's mind as he and John took the stand.

Four years later, the world looked on in horror as the danger of death to Olympic athletes became a reality, when eleven Israeli athletes were kidnapped from their dormitory by Arab guerrillas and eventually were killed. Some shortsighted people attempted to blame Tommie and John for introducing politics into the Olympic Games. But politics have always been a part of the Olympics. The United States shows its politicization in the opening ceremonies: it is the only country that doesn't dip its flag in honor of the home country's highest official. Nationalism plays a part in each victory ceremony as the victor's national anthem is played. The competitive tallying of gold, silver, and bronze medals between the United States and the USSR is another example of acceptable Olympic politics. Apparently only when political demonstrations which are unfavorable to the US are injected into the games do officials scream that the Olympics should not be used as a political tool. No one in America complains that the Olympics are political as black athletes win medals and symbolize that America is the land of equal opportunity. But when blacks attempt to use their athletic strength to claim their rights, they are being political.

The white establishment's phony antipolitical moralizing didn't dampen the emerging black attitudes. Black cultural heroes were born that day on the victory stand in Mexico City, and the black athletic revolution continued to grow after 1968. Black athletes created a climate around the country in which college administrations had to dismiss racist athletic directors and coaches to keep peace and continue fielding athletic teams. Black coaches were in demand by many colleges that wanted to appease black athletes. There was still a long way to go, but a revolution had started.

12

→》》《《←

Meanwhile, Where Were the Women?

The 1968 Olympic boycott was one of the biggest political events in the sports world during the highly political 1960s, and that Olympic October continued to generate controversy for years. But with all the excitement in the sports world and reams of press copy, few people noticed that the organizers of the boycott had been guilty of a glaring omission—women. Many of America's top women track and field athletes are black, but to my knowledge none were asked to join in planning or publicizing this effort to strike a blow for black freedom.

"What appalled me," said Olympic sprinter Wyomia Tyus, "was the fact that the men simply took us for granted. They assumed we had no minds of our own . . . that we would do whatever we were told to do. . . . I was never contacted. They didn't contact Edith Montgomery

[Olympic 200-meter sprinter], Madeline Manning [800-meter runner] or Barbara Ferrell [Olympic sprinter]."

Before the Olympics, reporters asked Tyus about her stand on the boycott, and since she knew nothing of the boycott plans other than what she read in the papers, she was at a loss for an answer. "All I could tell them was that I was training for the Olympic team," she recalls. "If I made the team, then if I were included in the discussion, I would see what kind of agreement we would all reach."

Tyus, along with many black athletes both male and female, had mixed feelings about the boycott. Most athletes had worked for years for this Olympic chance and hated the prospect of sacrificing it for an uncertain gain. Yet many felt strongly enough about the issues involved. Clearly, all black Olympians, male and female, should have been included in the planning and given an opportunity to make a choice.

"Basically, I was pretty ticked about the whole thing," Tyus says. And why shouldn't she be? Tyus was black and by any standard as serious an Olympic contender as Tommie Smith. Yet no one felt the need to solicit her support. No one had mentioned the boycott of the New York Athletic Club meet in New York to her. The boycott committee slighted all women when it implied that even within her own black community, Tyus was not a leader, despite her outstanding athletic achievements.

Boycott organizer Harry Edwards insists that the exclusion of black women was not intentional. The committee, he explains, knew that resources of time and money were limited, so it had to gather together the greatest political strength possible. Consequently, it sought support from America's best-known black athletes. Since women aren't well publicized, they aren't well known, and the advantage to be gained by securing their support is minimal.

Edwards assumed that the American Olympic fans would not be concerned if Edith Montgomery or Wyomia

Tyus failed to run in Mexico City but that they would be upset if John Carlos or Tommie Smith staged a boycott. Many male track fans have a built-in aversion to women who dare to be athletes anyway, and they would be just as happy to see the women stay at home rather than head to Mexico City with their track shoes. Edwards says that he would have accepted the women's support if they had come forward and offered to help. But the women, perhaps conscious of their secondary importance in the track world, waited to be asked.

Even after the athletes had assembled in Mexico City, Edwards's loyalists (Harry himself was not at the Games) never consulted the women about the boycott plans. Shortly before the Carlos and Smith protest demonstration, Tyus and Barbara Ferrell won first and third places in the 100 meters and took the victory stand in the rain to receive their medals. After Smith and Carlos had been ousted from Olympic Village, Tyus, acting on her own, chose to support the black power protest in press interviews and dedicated her gold medal to Tommie and John.

It would be easy—too easy—simply to blame Harry Edwards and his committee of organizers for overlooking the potential contribution of women to the boycott. The exclusion, however, reflects a much more complicated problem than the attitudes of just a few important men in the track world. Harry and his colleagues were acting realistically when they failed to consult women. Women athletes in this country are not considered full-status, legitimate athletes; consequently, they are not a powerful social force. Men are the *real* competitors in an American track meet; the women are looked on as specimens in a sideshow, and people don't care that much if they miss the sideshow.

Men are not the only ones guilty of underestimating women. At the price of their own self-esteem, women unconsciously absorb the attitudes of the society around them. I am a prime example. I had been working out with the men and now found myself identifying with them, developing a great disdain for the way "dumb broads" do things.

Given my athletic colleagues' view of women, it is not surprising that I geared my thinking toward the *real*—that is, male—athletes and didn't seriously consider my own athletic future. As I look back on it now, I find it ironic that although I strongly identified with the black struggle for equality in athletics and society, I never realized that women were victims of discrimination. I used my energy to join the black fight—in effect the black male fight since I knew few black women—and believed that I was part of an athletic revolution. I never considered the need for another revolution to help women athletes. I never thought to strike a blow against the sex discrimination that made my struggle to be a whole person—both woman and athlete—so difficult. I, like many women athletes, had been conditioned to accept second place. I now ask, "Where were the women in the Mexico City boycott?" I should also ask, "Where was I?"

The year 1968 was a good one for me. I broke through my lifetime best times in the 100-yard dash and the 220 at the San Jose State Invitational. Ideally, these accomplishments should have marked the beginning of a new push that would have carried me through to the AAU nationals and the Olympic Trials. Certainly, as 1968 began, I wanted very much to succeed. I wanted a piece of that "I'm special" feeling that's lavished so generously on men athletes and almost totally denied to women. I wanted recognition for my accomplishments, that "I am somebody," one-of-a-kind assurance. But how could I, as a woman athlete, get that feeling? I'd watch a well-organized men's meet in Modesto with thousands of spectators jamming the stands and lavish press coverage, then compete the next day in the Northern California Women's Championships on a high school dirt track before an audience of roughly fifty, mostly loyal parents and friends. No wonder I decided that the important athletes were men. No wonder I accepted the view that a woman, no matter how great she was, could only be the best *woman* sprinter or *woman* gymnast or *woman* jockey, because the *best* sprinter or jockey or gymnast was a man. Obviously the women's achievements weren't that significant. Gradually I became almost totally male-oriented as an athlete; the only way to get the flush of recognition I wanted was to become one of the guys. The female events were treated like fun and games. I wanted normal recognition, and that meant following the men.

Part of my problem was personal. After my disappointment about Billy Gaines, I moved to Santa Barbara to get away from the unpleasantness and humiliation I associated with the end of my junior year in San Jose. I felt I needed a new environment and new people to reorient myself and reestablish my sense of self-worth. So even though the track world had become the driving force of my life, I was sick of those Huey's Whorehouse stories and needed badly to get away.

So at a time in my career when I should have concentrated on achieving, I thought about escape. Perhaps my social situation was still more important to me than my athletic accomplishments, because fundamentally I knew that women weren't considered women if they were athletic but didn't have an active and accepted social life. The female stereotype could be stretched only so far, and I clearly had gone beyond the limits.

But as soon as I left the San Jose State track, my athletic ambitions collapsed. I took a summer job as a cocktail waitress in Santa Barbara to support myself. Naturally, no one on the job thought it was important enough for me to take a day off to compete in a track meet. The nontrack men I dated never took my athletic ambitions seriously. If I refused a date in order to work out, my date would answer, "But it can't be that important. You can miss it to go to this party." Even male athletes discounted my athletic goals. I worked out at the University of California, Santa Barbara, track and ran into some of the San Francisco '49ers who were at training camp there. As soon as the guys finished their practice, some of them would come over to the track adjoining their practice field and join me. The instant they arrived, fun replaced serious athletics. I wanted to be part of whatever they were doing, so I'd drop my workout and join them. They always knew I would; my workout couldn't be that important. And if they had a picnic or a trip up to the lake in mind, I gave up my own training program immediately.

My involvement with AAU track fizzled as I sought desperately to justify myself socially. The prestige of dating several '49ers did a lot more for my self-esteem and my public image than working out on the track did. I drifted further and further away from the women's track scene and didn't compete in the state or national AAU meets that year. To stay in national-caliber shape a runner must compete constantly to maintain a physical and mental competitive edge, and I was busy being female.

Perhaps if the newspapers had devoted as much attention to the women's nationals as they gave to the men's, I would have been drawn back to track, because at that point I definitely was in search of my own brand of glamour and recognition. Actually I did go where the newspapers pointed me. A girlfriend and I headed for Lake Tahoe, where the men's track team held its trials at the high-altitude center; and while the men thought about their Olympic ambitions, I thought about the men. Tahoe, a beautiful resort area, was the place where things were happening. (Meanwhile the women's Olympic trials were being held at some dusty God-forsaken town in New Mexico.) I found it easier to be on the edge of the big time by being associated with men than by struggling for my own stardom in a shadow. I looked on my own missed opportunities with only a twinge of regret.

By the time I returned to San Jose State for my senior year I was barely an athlete. Instead of running hard, hard workouts five times a week as I'd done in the years before, I slipped into easy, twice-a-week practices with the women's track team. There was no way I could get in shape on that schedule, but I had decided to skip the AAU schedule of meets in the upcoming year and remain a star in the small-time intercollegiate circuit. Occasionally I did work out with the men on the SJS track and learned how far I'd slipped physically. I'd forget that I wasn't in as good shape as I used to be, and I would drain myself completely trying to keep up. But training with the men did restore my spirits. I regained some of that proud self-confidence that overflowed from all of them.

I was one of the guys . . . and yet I wasn't. They accepted me in their workouts as much as they could, but they were still much faster than I could ever be. Relying on the men for good workouts gave me a false picture of my own ability. I never got a realistic conception of my speed or talent because I never was able to compare myself with other serious women runners. And I took from the men an attitude toward the big time that gave me illusions of a grandeur that I was never able to find. During workouts I may have given my all every day, but when it came to planning my life, I reined myself in to a fairly tight female stereotype; and when my drive for athletic excellence left me feeling like a "jock" or a neuter, I sacrificed my own goals to that stereotype.

Even when given opportunities for personal triumph, I rarely rated my accomplishments as very important. At the Second Annual SJS Women's Invitational, I saw a chance to set a national collegiate record in the 50-yard dash. The Fresno Relays, a national men's meet, was scheduled for the same day; I figured I'd finish all my races in the morning and still make it to Fresno that evening for the *real* athletic event.

The schedule of events for the Invitational was badly

planned, at least for me. I had to run four races in a row: the semifinal of the 100-yard dash, the semifinal of my 50, the final of the 100, and then the final of the 50. I could handle the physical output—I had done plenty of harder workouts—but I found it difficult to get myself psyched up for each race. By the time of the last race, I wasn't at all sure whether I wanted to run or not. My ride wanted to leave for Fresno and was getting impatient because my meet was running an hour behind schedule. My legs were starting to stiffen, and I wasn't sure I could make a strong attempt at the record anyway. I decided against the race, packed up my gear, and climbed into the Fresno-bound Volkswagen. Then, just as we were pulling out, I heard the announcement for the 50-yard final.

"Wait!" I yelled to the driver. "Just hang around for six seconds, okay?" I jumped out of the car and made it to the starting blocks just in time for the gun. Six seconds later I was co-holder of the national collegiate record, a record that would be retired that year because the 50 would be dropped from the collegiate circuit.

That night in Fresno I felt totally justified as I prowled the streets with the guys looking for action. We owed it to ourselves to have a wild time, I thought, after being such terrific physical specimens that day. Back at San Jose, I learned that I'd been on a special pass that night in Fresno. We'd had fun, but now the men expected me to conform to the passive female role. I couldn't love 'em and leave 'em, standard operating procedure for the guys. When I started looking for fun, the ugly stories started up again to put me in my place. The men had been outdoing me in the partying, high-living life for a long time, but they wanted me to know that the fast life was a male-only domain. Women weren't supposed to enjoy the same freedom. After all, they were the victims that made the men's freedom possible.

Although I imitated the men socially, I was substituting just their style for real substance on the track. Men were my only role models, so naturally I assumed that I was the female version of Tommie Smith or John Carlos. Only in personality was I able to emulate them. I had always loved Billy's stories of these tough athletes' tricks to psych each other out just before the gun. Actual conversations would take place between the "Runners come to your marks" and the "Set": "I'm gonna smoke y'all today," Billy might say to Carlos as they climbed into the blocks. "Hell, I'll save you a piece of the tape after I get there," John would flash back.

Soon, I too was strutting around the women's track as I tried to make my own women's meets seem important by relating them to the men's athletic events. When I ran against Deanne Kurth Carlsen from Chico State—my first real competition in a long time—I convinced myself of the importance of the confrontation by telling myself that our race was just like the Tommie Smith–Jimmy Hines duel that was raging over the number one spot in the men's 220 that year. Carlsen, a nationally ranked hurdler, won. This was the first time I had lost in intercollegiate competition, but I reconciled myself to the defeat, saying that, after all, Tommie lost races too.

With 'Los and Gaines as my new models for track behavior, the polite Smith manner I had adopted earlier turned into a loud brashness. I made it clear that like the men I could do everything wrong the night before a meet and still win. I'd seen John Carlos down a fifth of Scotch the night before setting a world record, and I'd seen these guys have two or three women coming and going out of their rooms the nights before and after their meet. So I always partied before a meet and showed up just in time to mess up my bed and look like I'd been there when wake-up call came. "I'm the John Carlos of this team," I told myself. "I can get away with anything just like him, because they need me." I always had to compare myself with a male to feel important. *Male athletes* seemed to mean virile, sexy, and desirable

Patty Van Wolvelaere and I work out on a California beach.
CREDIT: Micki McGee/ISSS

while *female athletes* seemed to mean unattractive, without poise, and undesirable. But why did I learn to scorn women's athletics as not real? Why did I decide that I'd rather have the reflected limelight with the men than commit myself to my own track career? (Often I would run exhibition races in well-publicized and well-attended men's meets rather than compete in an important, but poorly attended women's meet.) As I look back on my experience I realize that I am responsible for my own lack of direction. However, I also think that everything around me conspired to reinforce my tendency to have a male orientation. I wasn't the only one focused on men; the whole sports world treated male primacy as a law of nature.

The only women who were ever considered serious athletes were the Olympic contenders. A woman who didn't have that Olympic certification was viewed either as a dilettante or a failure. That meant that only a few women in the entire country ever had a chance of recognition; the second string of potential stars never made the sports news. Roy Jefferson of the Washington Redskins once said to me, "You're like me—just one of the guys on the team, but your friend Patty Van Wolvelaere is like the Sonny Jurgensen." Roy didn't realize one thing: in women's track, the Roy Jeffersons are unknown entities and the Sonny Jurgensens are barely recognized. I think I decided that the recognition I was getting for my energy output wasn't enough to make the struggle worthwhile.

The track world gave me plenty of evidence for that conclusion. Women ran in front of large enthusiastic crowds only when the meets were coed. But together did not necessarily mean equal; women usually ran three or four events to the men's twenty or more. And with the press and spectator attention focused on the men, women often encountered a condescending attitude from officials. Mary Decker, one of America's best middle-distance runners, was once forced off the track by an official who told her, "You don't belong on the track now, little girl." If Decker's coach had not intervened, she would have missed the race in which she set a new world record in the 1000 yards.

Many of the women's AAU meets I attended were rinky-dink. Many times, parents and spectators were snatched out of the stands to serve as timers and officials. It seemed to me that very often AAU officials sent to oversee women's events were subpar. Take the women's sprint medley relay I participated in during my first indoor nationals in Oakland in 1968. The first leg of the relay is 440 yards, followed by two 110s, then anchored by a 220 runner. Since the indoor track is only 160 yards around, the first runners had to complete two and two-thirds laps before handing off to the first 110 runner, who then ran less than a lap to hand off to the second one. I was the third runner, and I stood cheering our leadoff quarter-miler on. She was running well, but I could tell she was tiring. She still had to run past me and another 50 yards to where our second runner was waiting. But Split Lynch, an AAU official who is a fixture in the track world, obviously wasn't paying much attention to our event and ordered me and the other third leg runners to get onto the track to receive the baton. I knew Lynch was wrong, but in the excitement of the moment, we had our adrenalin going and jumped onto the track anyway. I grabbed the baton from our quarter-miler and ran a whole lap, wondering where my 110 was supposed to end. Finally I realized that I had been running all by myself; the other girls had been told to stop because the race had been run improperly.

Carlos kidded me about that later. "You shouldn't-a stopped. You was winnin'." But as it turned out, the second time around, we didn't have a chance of winning. The officials decided to run the race again only a half hour later, and our 440 runner simply wasn't strong enough to do it again that soon. We didn't even qualify to the semifinals; yet if our 440 runner had been able to run well, we were expected to compete.

Poor organization is only one of many examples of the track world's double standard when it comes to men and women. Many times I've seen Billy Gaines go home from a track meet with a television, a tape player, or a stereo after winning the 60-yard dash. Yet Patty Van Wolvelaere or Cherrie Sherrard, both top hurdlers, received bouquets of roses after their victories.

(Women never shared in the hustles that enable men

athletes to survive. Most of the women Olympians were given track shoes, but they never received the full run of the line that Billy Gaines or John Carlos enjoyed. These men came away with hundreds of dollars' worth of equipment, and the managers knew perfectly well that much of the gear would be sold. Apparently Puma or Adidas didn't think that women were worth an equally big investment. Shoes were a minor hustle compared to the other luxuries men took for granted. Alumni fans provided Mickey Mouse jobs for men, but seldom thought that women athletes also need to eat. Cars, scholarships, and money under the table went to successful male athletes, whereas the best women were given no choice but to run for fun.)

Women college and AAU track athletes also knew that their sport offered them little future. At that time there was no professional track. Because of media prejudices, a top woman athlete could not turn a successful sports career into a job as a sportscaster or product spokeswoman. Maybe sports fans take out their wallets when they learn that a Joe Namath wears Super Seducer Aftershave, but no adman saw the possibilities of product endorsements by Olympians Wyomia Tyus or Olga Connolly. Because women's college athletic programs were badly funded, top women athletes couldn't even look forward to coaching a viable athletic team. The best they could hope to do was teach physical education, a career that at the time didn't really hit the spot for a women with highly competitive instincts.

The male–female double standard is also in evidence when AAU officials decide to legislate the athletes' personal lives. When men's and women's teams tour internationally, the women have curfews, but the men go to bed when (and where) they choose. One male runner was caught in a woman competitor's room one night during the 1970 European tour. The woman was shipped home and banned from international competition for one year, whereas the man escaped with a verbal reprimand. This example is not unique; generally the double standard is strictly enforced.

Thus when we ask why black women athletes were not more of a political force in 1968, we must remember the problems that confronted, and in many cases still confront, all women athletes. Throughout their sports careers women have to battle pressures that no athlete should have to face—a social attitude that denies their legitimacy, a poorly organized competitive structure, and the failure of our institutions to recognize and encourage their achievements. Some outstanding and unusually determined women have managed to overcome these obstacles and achieve athletic triumphs. But as the 1968 boycott proved, even these women are not given the leadership roles they deserve. And most of us aren't Superwoman. I offer myself as an example of those who fell by the wayside. I'm not particularly proud of the way my track ambitions collapsed in 1968, but I also know that I was not unique.

13

❧ ⟫⟫ ⟪⟪ ❧

Imitation Athlete

A trip to Europe after graduation from San Jose State showed me that a woman athlete's life could be different. Although European women obviously are not as fast or as strong as their male colleagues, they are not considered the second-class citizens of sport. A young East German woman athlete didn't know what I meant when I asked how she dealt with the stigma of being a woman athlete; she was also genuinely shocked to learn of the attitudes and training inequities in the United States. Most eastern European countries have combined teams in which men and women train together and receive equal coaching and medical attention. These athletes can share hints on technique and gain psychological strength from one another, and no one seems to think that the women athletes are weird, neuter, or unfeminine.

Unfortunately my own athletic aspirations were so confused at that point that I failed to become very inspired. The American girls I traveled with in Europe had men on their minds, and so did I. I even managed to break my own carefully cultivated addiction to physical exercise despite two weeks of actual physical pain as my body complained about its lack. I gained weight and passively watched my body become a liability rather than an instrument of expression. I was disgusted with myself and at the same time was unable to reassert the part of me I liked.

I realized how lazy I'd become when I ran into the U.S. national track and field team in Stuttgart, West Germany. I got a charge from watching John Carlos, the man the press pilloried as the villain in the Mexico City Olympics, play up to the German crowds. John doesn't speak a word of German, but being a master comedian, he crossed the language barrier. He challenged the Germans to competitions in anything—beer drinking, arm wrestling—and then he made up the rules as he went along. John was the star athlete. I soaked up some of that attention by partying with him that weekend, but I wanted more than just to be *with* John, I wanted to *be* him. I longed to experience the satisfaction—in both mind and body—that he was feeling. The excitement of his life compared to mine hit home as I felt, with real physical pain, a purposelessness as I wandered through Europe.

Five months later I was back at San Jose State to get a master's degree and found myself in the worst physical shape of my life. The other track athletes were doing sprint form drills to get ready for the indoor season, while I could hardly push myself around the track. But after six months of boycotting my body in Europe, I was determined to get back that athletic side of my life. So I joined the workouts as if I had been training all along.

My legs fought back. The human body needs an adequate amount of background work before it can demand a high-level performance of muscles, tendons, and connective tissues. The subtle, underlying strength of the body must be formed before the muscles are ready for the rapid-fire contractions required for top-speed sprinting. With no coach to help me program a comeback workout, I ignored my body's needs, pushed ahead to sprint work long before I was ready, and my crash program crashed. I put on my spikes and was trying to sprint after only a week of jogging. My leg muscles and tendons simply weren't prepared to take the strain. I damaged my Achilles tendon just above my left heel so badly that I could hardly walk, let alone run. Whenever I tried to use it, that tendon creaked and caused tremendous pain throughout the rest of the track season.

So I became an imitation athlete. Periodically I took my mushy, out-of-shape legs back to the track, but now I was a mere jogger. I couldn't even look at the workouts. The smell of liniment, the sight of those powerful hamstring muscles contracting, the intensity of those athletic moments of truth—everything I loved about track hurt me now that I had to view the sport as a spectator.

All the time my body failed me, I was on my own. I discovered over the years, especially as I got older, that most people would barely react to a woman athlete's injury. Their attitude always was one of "Oh, well, now you can go back to being a girl." No thought is ever given to the mental anguish a woman athlete experiences when her identity is wrapped inside a plaster cast. However, the masses understand the psychological pain of a Joe Namath when his knee is operated on and he can't play in a big game.

Of course financial factors enter into management's extreme care of a costly athlete, but an injured player's state of mind is usually considered by his friends. Not so with the woman athlete. A male athlete's smallest malfunction is given enormous care, but no one in the SJS physical education departments seemed at all interested in my injury. Eventually I got some help by using my trusty cheer-leader personality. I was injured physically, but my female manipulative skills were in top shape. The equipment manager let me in to use the whirlpool when the men were out on the field. The trainer for the men's teams agreed to give me a supportive tape job for my foot each day so I could run on the injured foot to begin strengthening it. None of the other women had these facilities and, miffed by their lack of interest, I gloated over my ability to get what they couldn't.

(I later learned that disregard for a woman athlete's injury is not uncommon, no matter how good she is. Jan Svendsen underwent two knee operations to correct an injury she sustained while representing the United States in a meet against the USSR. Although she had been on an American team when injured, Jan had to rehabilitate her knee on her own and struggle with Medi-Cal bills and insurance problems for two years before even part of her debt was paid by medical and AAU insurance. She survived this episode as an athlete only because of her tremendous strength and dedication.)

My injury pretty well finished my track career that year, so I took a part-time job as a waitress at St. James Infirmary, a local college hang-out, and I found myself in a new kind of contest. Sawdust on the floor, huge barrels of peanuts, and crazy taped music—everything from Irish jigs to the Supremes—created a fun atmosphere, and I convinced myself that this bar was the main show in town and I was the star. All the managers and bartenders were running games on the waitresses, emotionally and sexually, so I decided I wouldn't be the next in their line of victims. I listened to their "dirt stories" (they loved to brag about whom they had conquered the night before), and then I'd top them with one of my own. "And mine are famous athletes," I'd say. "Who are you talking about, smartass?"

I became a monster who could out-talk, out-run, outdrink, out-swear, and out-anything anybody. Guys would bet me three pitchers of beer that I couldn't do thirty push-ups.

"Pour those pitchers," I hollered as I whipped off the push-ups. I was top athlete in the place. Everybody made a big deal about it—especially me. If anyone dared to suggest that he was athletic, I'd challenge him.

"You must do *something* with legs like that," was a usual opening line.

"Yep, I can outdo you at anything," I boasted.

"Yeah? What have you got in mind?"

"You name it and I'll beat you."

I was a sure winner in an arm-wrestling contest. All I had to do was hold the dude's arm straight up and the crowd conceded the match to me—any man should be able to beat a girl at arm wrestling. I surprised lots of guys who were sure no girl could beat him in a sprint—even when he was overweight and half drunk. And for my grand finale, I'd empty 100-pound sacks of peanuts into the storage loft over the bar. That drew "oo's" and "ah's" from the crowd every time. I was a mean and quick-tongued woman. I had reverse machismo at its worst. I was the jock of St. James Infirmary—*Screwy Huey, Superstar!*

One Sunday afternoon in Sausalito my barroom athleticism reached its peak when I ran into my favorite Philadelphia Eagle. We started drinking beer at Zack's, a popular bayfront spot, then switched to shots of tequila, and by late afternoon we were feeling no pain.

Suddenly my friend snatched me out of my chair. "C'mon," he said. "You're going to race this guy over here."

"You're crazy, too," I answered.

But he was persuasive, and the next thing I knew I was kicking off my shoes and doing a few hamstring stretches for the crowd that was gathering out front in the parking lot. It looked like I was stuck with this race, so I figured I might as well do it right. I went into my act—my John Carlos strut.

"C'mon, give me a foot for a starting block."

My friend walked over and placed a foot near the starting line that we had marked off in the gravel—that's right, gravel. I took one practice start and suddenly the crowd realized that this could actually be a race. The odds, which had been about 10 to 1 against me, changed drastically. My friend grabbed me back to the starting line.

"What'd'ya do that for?" he whispered. "I already had $200 on ya and now I won't be able to get many more bets. You weren't 'spozed to show 'em you could run."

"Two hundred dollars! Lord, now I've really got to run!" I said.

People emptied from the bar onto the parking lot, where the competition and I were lined up. I was too drunk to get nervous or even feel that gravel on my bare feet. Naturally there were several false starts with people just clowning around. The crowd kept growing bigger.

When the race finally started, I blitzed out of my make-shift starting block and zoomed to the finish line with a grandstand lean where the tape should have been. I never even saw my competition. He slipped about two steps out and was never able to catch me.

I was so thankful. I never could have looked my Eagle friend straight in the eye if I'd let him lose his $200 bet. We kept drinking and eating for the rest of that night and woke up the next morning in a hotel not knowing what town we were in or how we'd gotten there.

14

→>> «←

From the Ghetto to Cowtown

As I drove home from work I could see two of the students from my gymnastics class hustling—those pretty, dark-skinned bodies for sale to make a few bucks to survive. Soon afterward I learned that the brother of one of my students had been killed the night before—shot in a fight. A week or so later, my favorite cutie freshman was sentenced to ten years for armed robbery.

These were my students at Federal City College in Washington, D.C., a public, four-year college with an open-door policy and a $29-a-quarter tuition fee. Our building, the physical education facilities, was on the corner of 16th and Q Streets, N.W., right in the heart of one of Washington's ghettos.

Federal City was my first teaching assignment and the beginning of a string of battles with traditional physical education. In this ghetto school, I learned that I had to free myself from the values I'd acquired as a p.e. student if I wanted to do any constructive teaching. My training hadn't prepared me to deal with what I saw at FCC; instead, I found it had given me nothing but a cumbersome set of useless attitudes. (Later, I took my liberated head back to middle-class schools and found myself battered against the stone wall of the status quo.)

My FCC students were good people trapped by circumstances, doing their best to survive and willing to use any means they found necessary. Their personal stories amazed me—twelve kids in a two-bedroom flat, no heat, a blind mother, a father who hadn't been seen in years. Here I was screaming at them about their homework when they were lucky to make it to school alive. Obviously I had a lot to learn about teaching in the ghetto, and the training I'd received from the San Jose State physical education department was about as valuable as a bottle of Coppertone in the middle of a Washington winter.

I came to Federal City almost by accident. Just before the school year began I received a call offering me a $10,000 a year job in the physical education department. I had sent them a resume, but when the application form from them had arrived, I threw it away, disinterested. Now, the eagerness of the recruiter should have warned me that FCC hadn't exactly been deluged by applicants for the job. But I'd been having trouble with the SJS p.e. department over my master's degree and as a result wasn't yet qualified for most teaching jobs. FCC, however, was willing to take me one step short of my officially receiving an M.A. As much as I hated to leave the west coast beach life, I knew that the East could hold a lot of new people and adventures, so I eagerly headed across the country.

My first day as a Federal City professor went well as I filled in the personnel department's papers and met with the administrators and other teachers. When I went to the restroom and glanced in the mirror, it finally dawned on me: this was the only white face I'd seen all day. I panicked.

Fortunately, many of my fellow teachers were new and we clung together for security. Edna Long, from Chicago, the new dance instructor, also in her first year of teaching, became my best friend. That first day she commented on the trouble she'd been having with some of the secretaries at the school.

"I thought maybe they were prejudiced against me," I said. "It's a relief to know they're just naturally nasty."

"From what I hear, the students will be pretty rough on us, too," Edna said. "I was feeling shaky about this whole job, but my daddy told me, 'You're as black as they are. Don't let them scare you off.'"

Terrific, I thought. Where does that leave me?

My first job was adjusting to chilly Washington after sunny California. I moved into an apartment in Edna's building in southwest Washington and met the cockroaches. There were thousands of them. I didn't mind so much having them around, but I hated *seeing* them. Each morning I yelled, "Okay, roaches, I'm coming into the bathroom! Get lost!" and waited to hear those feet tick-tick-ticking out of sight before I turned on the light. Then I'd announce, "I'm going to open the medicine cabinet. Please, don't be in there." I'd rattle the cabinet door and give them plenty of time to scramble to safety. Some evenings, I tried to concentrate on a conversation with my guests while the roaches threw the silverware off the kitchen counter and into the sink. Distracting.

It wasn't only the roaches that amazed this California beach freak. The ability of the Washingtonians to turn off their physical lives and go into hibernation for the winter was equally foreign. I thrived on physical exercise, and suddenly I had no playmates. I managed to stir a few friends out of their winter's snooze, but when California dreaming totally overcame me, I'd create my own little bit of the beach. I hooked up my sunlamp, sat in my beach chair, wriggled my feet in a box of sand I'd brought with me from the West Coast and cried as I looked out the window at the rain. I played side one of Carol King's "Tapestry" album as I sat there contemplating the pouring sleet and rain. She sang about cold and rain and being far from home. Her music was talking to me.

I didn't have too much time for homesickness during the school day; my students had plenty of tricks to keep me occupied. The first day I showed up to teach Introduction to Physical Education I was mentally geared up for a confrontation. I had learned from my SJS classes that the first day of class was the teacher's make-it or break-it day. I had stayed up the night before preparing my dynamic first lesson and was all psyched up to do battle as I walked into the class. Actually, *picked* my way into the class is more accurate: the building was undergoing a renovation that should have been done the month before, which left the building in complete disarray for the first month of classes. Construction materials were scattered all over; men were hammering all day, making instruction next to impossible; and most students could barely find the right classrooms. When I finally found my room and fought my way inside, it was empty. I waited anxiously because I didn't know what I was supposed to do next. I knew what the model p.e. teacher did, but my empty classroom didn't match up to those textbook directions. Eventually a few students casually strolled in, but by that time I didn't know what to do with myself, let alone them. When the class period was over, about ten students had cruised in, looked quizzically at me, grabbed their assignments and left after a word or two.

To tell the truth I was relieved. That first week of non-school allowed me to get used to my students and them to get used to seeing me. We needed it. Thanks to Tommie Smith and the Speed City Gang, I'd already had a little black conditioning. I thought I knew how to talk black English, but even *I* needed an interpreter with some of these FCC characters. Even when I did understand, I often demanded that my students use white English. I insisted that jargon didn't belong in a college classroom—a theory that left me constantly frustrated as I tried to apply a standard of English to students who weren't interested.

I soon saw that many of my students were all but illiterate. In high school I had wondered who got the zeros and 10 percents on the nationwide aptitude tests. Now I found out. The District of Columbia seemed to have a monopoly on the lowest scores. That doesn't mean the kids were dumb. By no means; they had a lot of "slick potential"—basic intelligence that all inner-city youngsters have to learn to develop just to stay alive and well. But they hadn't been taught any of the basic skills that the rest of America expects from its students. Had there been a nationwide "slick potential" test, these kids would've gotten the 99 percent scores, and my friends and I in suburban San Jose would have gotten the zeros. But it wasn't that way.

My students had been passed through the Washington school system year after year unable to spell much more than their own names. They couldn't add up the prices on a grocery list. They had no chance of writing a grammatically correct sentence. When high school finished with them they came to rock-bottom-cheap Federal City and squeezed out enough course points to become teachers and go back into the system that created them. No wonder there was a vicious circle of nonlearning.

With the first set of papers turned in to me, I saw the problem in black and white—"Wuz" . . . "Iny" . . . "Fone." They did their best to spell the words the way they sounded, but English doesn't happen to be that way. I decided to make my lessons simpler and concrete, and I prepared assignment sheets with an example of every possible thing my students would need to know in order to do the homework. I failed to realize that to understand the assignment they had to be able to read it. Some of them simply couldn't read, and most of the rest saw no need to follow directions.

As I look back on that class, I'm ashamed of the way I hassled those students, trying to make them fit my WASP standards. Just turning in a piece of paper with their handwriting on it was a major accomplishment for some of these kids, and I didn't know that I should be praising them for doing the first homework of their lives. Instead, I criticized them for failing to meet college-level academic standards.

My attitude toward Federal City grew progressively worse as every educational value I learned at SJS was turned inside out. The SJS p.e. teachers had emphasized the need for discipline, but I had to be cool and deal with the FCC students on their own terms. I loaned a copy of a textbook to one of my students who couldn't afford his own book. In class one day I asked to borrow the book back for the period. Before handing it to me, he leafed through the book and pulled out four joints of marijuana. I tried my damndest not to react. No eating, no gum-chewing—those were the disciplinary rules we had talked about in my SJS classes. I had always chewed gum and brought candy to the class. I figured that a few joints at FCC were like gum and candy at SJS and I let the incident slide. Perhaps I didn't see any reason to get excited because at Federal City many of the teachers needed more discipline than the students. Many mornings I was the only teacher in the p.e. building. This only reinforced the students' irresponsibility. I had been the absentee queen of my classes at SJS, but now I was responsible; I knew that I had to pull myself out of bed in the morning and get to class just in case two students showed up, proud that they had their work done. I couldn't let them down. If I had simply canceled the class without warning, these students wouldn't spend the time and effort to be disappointed a second time.

After a few months at Federal City, I was shocked to find myself becoming a racist. Actually that was very easy to do; racism is rampant in Washington. Very little social mixing between black and white was done, unlike my experience at San Jose. The racism was strong from both sides. I went to Howard University to watch my friend Edna dance one night, and I felt contempt in the stares directed my way.

"Don't let me hear you cryin'," Edna said when I told her how uncomfortable I'd been. "For twenty-four years you've been on the other side of racism. Don't complain because for one night you have to deal with the side I face nearly everywhere I go."

Gradually I came to terms with the race issue. In my fit of racism I had concluded that "these lazy, ignorant niggers" had created this nasty ghetto. Now I realized that I should have blamed the social structure that allowed such poverty and oppression. I decided to stop worrying about my white SJS values and start relating to my students' lives.

My ghetto English improved so that I could communicate with my students instead of merely talking *at* them. I threw out the traditional p.e. curriculum and started to chose materials that my students could understand. I gave them Dr. Bruce Ogilvie's articles on sport and personality. This aspect of the psychology of sport they could relate to. We discussed our experiences in peak moments of competition or exertion and the possibilities of understanding more about ourselves through physical movement. At last I saw my students come to life. We were talking about their experiences, not the thirty-year-old ideas of white theoreticians of physical education. No, my students didn't suddenly become articulate speakers and accomplished writers. But they were learning something, and so was I. I no longer went into each class expecting my students to be ignorant and proving myself right.

I now tried to make my classes relevant to their lives. In Safety Education, I had been teaching everything straight

This was my track class at Federal City College. I think we taught each other a lot.

CREDIT: Quintin Carter

from the book, a book that made no sense at all in the inner city. There I was, trying to get across safety rules and health factors to ghetto students, many of whom were the same people that my safety education book warned against. They were the ones ripping people off the best they could because they didn't have anything. Obviously all my students knew more about staying alive and safe than any book did. Instead of preaching those unrealistic bits of advice, I was determined to do whatever I could to meet their real needs. If they couldn't write sentences, I'd teach them to write sentences. If they couldn't spell, I'd teach them to use the dictionary. I no longer insisted that white English was right and black English wrong. I explained that white English was the language of the dominant culture in America and they would have to learn it if they wanted to get to play in the game.

I took my students to the Library of Congress and taught them how to use a card catalog. Most of them had never done any research before, but in my class they were surprised to learn that they actually could write term papers. In an activity class, I brought men and women together in coed track and field. In the spring we borrowed the Georgetown University track and twenty of us hopped onto the bus at Federal City and joked our way across town. "It may be sprinkling at Federal City," someone said, "but you *know* it ain't gonna rain on no white folks' heads over there at Georgetown. We safe." "Oh, sorry," another student said, remembering that one of us was white. Then they realized they had no need to apologize; I had lived their life in the ghetto long enough to identify with them, not the affluent Georgtowners.

Teaching the men and women together was beneficial for all concerned. The men were wary of me at first because most of them had never had a woman teach them anything athletic, but as soon as they realized that I knew my stuff, they were fine. The men learned more quickly than the women because as boys they had learned a larger repertoire of basic movement skills. They willingly helped the women learn skills and gain confidence. Their example strengthened my belief in the desirability of coed physical education, especially at the level of basic skills.

By the time I'd adjusted to Federal City and found several playmates to replace my California gang, the school year was about over. In a depressed mood, I had handed in my resignation that April; now I wanted to stay. But the department chairman explained to me that he didn't feel he could count on my decision to stay as being final. What would he do if I found I was too comfortable in my California summer and when September rolled around he was one p.e. teacher short?

I headed back to California and began teaching at California Polytechnic State University in San Luis Obispo. My assignment was to coach the women's track and field team and to teach the Methods of Teaching Track and Field course for physical education majors. In addition, I taught several activity classes for the general student body. At Cal Poly I returned to traditional physical education and found I was as alienated as I'd ever been at FCC. I brought with me flexibility and spontaneity from FCC, but I learned that at Cal Poly not much mattered more than the rules. The most responsible physical educator at Federal City, I again found myself cast as the rebel.

Cal Poly teachers were expected to have every moment of class period planned in advance, and that hadn't been my style. I had had to improvise in a chaotic FCC environment. To change a class at Cal Poly, a teacher had to fill out the proper forms in triplicate in advance and get the department head's signature. To me, that meant that spur-of-the-moment creativity was out. When Tommie Lee White, world-class hurdler, stopped in at San Luis Obispo one day, I decided that my class should get the benefit of his expertise. My students lit up like light bulbs when Tommie Lee walked in and turned them on to hurdling. But I was reprimanded for that later. I hadn't informed the department that I had scheduled a guest lecturer.

Another time I decided to take advantage of a gorgeous day to let my track team train on a nearby beach. Again, I was supposed to have filled out those forms and gotten the department head's signature. But I couldn't predict that the weather would be good for a beach workout until the day came, so I just packed up my team and headed for the sand. Later, I realized that my failure to do the paperwork was only half the problem. In fact, the department head fundamentally disapproved of my choice of location. The beach represented fun, and evidently my athletes weren't supposed to enjoy themselves while training.

I had always disapproved of the fight that seemed to be part of education. I figured we were all trying to move in the same direction; why didn't we help each other? I also disliked the traditional "me teacher, you pupil" approach and wanted to treat my students as responsible adults. I knew there were gaps in my knowledge, so occasionally I would allow students who had expertise in a subject to take over the class. We all learned from each other that way and our classes were much more comfortable. I could well remember that at times I had been extremely frustrated at SJS because I knew more about a subject than one of my p.e. instructors, who continually shut me up and continued her own instruction. That wouldn't happen in my classes.

Coaching was the most challenging part of my job at Cal Poly. I had never realized the tremendous responsibility a coach assumes when she begins that first workout. The women on the team had different levels of skill, and I tried to create individual workouts for each. In addition, I was the team's trainer, treating injuries and monitoring my athletes' physical condition. (Unlike the men's athletic department, the women's had no funds for a trainer.) Most of the athletes on my team knew nothing about track, and I had to teach them the fundamentals. Why hadn't their high schools taught them the basics? I wondered. Had nothing changed since I was in school? Apparently not.

There was plenty of natural talent on my team, and as the year started I hoped to build one of the best women's intercollegiate track teams in the country. Five of my athletes had experience in AAU clubs and were eager to run for Cal Poly. Our early practices were promising; then my hopes collapsed abruptly: four of my potential stars became academically ineligible. I was furious with myself for failing to make sure that they were keeping their grades up. Why hadn't I set up the same academic security network that the male coaches used to protect their athletes? I should have known more than anyone else how to keep my athletes eligible. As a student at San Jose State, I often bailed out male athletes who had problems with their grades. I just plain forgot. I knew the eligibility rules were nonsense—many of the male athletes should have been ineligible by any honest standard—but I assumed that my girls would stay eligible in the same semidishonest way. I soon learned that female athletes aren't given the same courtesies that the almighty campus superstars are given.

My athletes, unlike the men, were not supplied with tutors. They worked part-time while the men picked up scholarship checks. My women had to adhere to the same standards without getting the same advantages. My efforts to pull strings for my athletes failed. Male p.e. teachers who regularly bailed out their athletes with a few extra grade points treated me like a particularly repellant beggar. One of my hurdlers, Janet Benford, had a 1.9 grade point average, but needed a 2.0 to compete. The same instructor who had helped his male athletes by allowing them to do extra work when their grades were below standard refused to consider giving the same privilege to my hurdler. His obstinacy was tragic for Janet. If she had remained eligible for the college meets, this hurdler had an excellent prospect of taking one of the top two places at the national track and field championship meet of the Association for Intercollegiate Athletics for Women. A victory there could have led to a place on the U.S. Student World Games team that competed in Moscow that August. Had a man's National Collegiate Athletic Association championship attempt been on the line, I think his male instructor might have thought twice about helping him.

This condescending attitude toward women in sport was

common among male coaches. One day I was helping a new sprinter learn to start and decided to let her get comfortable her own way in the starting blocks before I made corrections. Suddenly a voice screamed at me from across the track, "Is that any way to teach her how to start?" I left her and confronted my male critic in my best Federal City style. "Show some respect, mutha-fucka," I snapped. "I don't need your disrespectful comments to me or my athletes."

That surprised him. He became instantly polite. "I just thought maybe I could help. I went to Stanford and learned starts from Payton Jordon, one of the best sprint coaches in the country."

"Fine," I answered. "I went to San Jose State and learned the Bud Winter rocket start from the master himself."

Yet after a while, I came to understand why many male coaches have a low opinion of women coaches' training techniques and knowledge. At nearly every track meet I attended with my team, I saw women coaches who were totally unqualified for their jobs. Usually their administrators had to put someone in charge of the team and had just picked a staff member at random. They were doing their best with the fundamental knowledge of track they'd managed to pull together from their careers as physical education students. But most of them had never been involved as serious athletes in any sport, and they lacked the track instinct that is acquired after years of involvement. The fault lies not with these women but with the system of creating physical educators to teach basic skills but not coaches to deal with high-level athletics. Until we develop more women athletes—actual athletes and not just participants in low-level track and field playday—and assign them coaching responsibilities, our young girls will not have the opportunity to learn from women who really know their sport.

Today many of the top coaches of women's track teams

are men, but I believe that women coaches have special
insights into the female personality and experience to offer
women athletes. For example, most girls have not been
toughened to the win-strive-conquer attitudes that are ingrained in so many male athletes from early childhood; as
a result, they have to be treated less roughly—they simply
are not used to the militaristic approach to which many
young men are exposed. Girls tend to be less confident in
their movement patterns initially, simply because they
haven't had as great a variety of physical experiences as
boys. This lack of athletic background makes coaching a
women's team a complex and formidable assignment. With
every intercollegiate team I've coached I've had to deal
with a few athletes who are confident of their physical
talents and are ready to have them challenged, as well as
with many girls who are participating in the sport for the
first time. The neophytes have never pushed their bodies
to the point of fatigue and pain, secure in the knowledge
that tomorrow they'll be stronger for the exertion, and
many are afraid of the feeling. Many are afraid of attempting new skills. Learning to use one's physical self for the
first time is an awakening, and I think women coaches can
understand and empathize with their athletes' doubts and
fears and help conquer them more readily than men, who
are used to experienced athletes.

Whenever I coach an untrained woman athlete, I love to
see her tentative movements turn to sure ones, to see her
perform with confidence. It is up to women coaches to help
these emerging athletes believe that their strong bodies are
beautiful, that they should be proud of an athletic body. We
have to give them faith so they can fight off the wave of
stereotyped "femininity," so that they can find out, as I
have, that physical strength is the source of much mental
strength.

The new militant woman coach is not likely to settle for
second-best for her athletes. Many coaches and officials

seem to assume that women by nature are fated to get by with less—poor facilities, lower budgets, less prestige. The new breed of woman coach is more willing to demand that their athletes be treated with respect. I came face to face with the problem of lack of respect for women athletes several years later when I coached the women's volleyball team at Mira Costa College in Oceanside, California. I was elated to get the chance to build the first women's intercollegiate athletic team on the campus, but I soon came to realize that women athletes were still the second-class citizens of sport.

The message became clear when my team was asked to play a match at Imperial Valley College the afternoon before a men's nighttime football game. My immediate reaction to the double-decker plan was negative: "We're not going to be anybody's girlie sideshow entertainment before the *real* athletic contest." Against my better judgement, I was convinced to take my team. As usual, I should have trusted my instincts.

The Imperial Valley coach and I agreed to play a best three out of five game match. MCC lost the first game, but in the middle of the second game, my inexperienced players had recovered from their initial stage fright and had their adrenalin flowing. We lost the second game in extended play and were eager to come back and try for the next three wins. We were clearly the better team, but we had taken a long time to get going. Then, before we could start the third game, a voice barked over the loudspeaker, "Okay, everybody grab a chair and clear the gym please. The football team is on their way in for practice."

"What?" I shouted. I received an explanation that confirmed my worst nightmares. The Imperial Valley football team ran drills in the gym four hours before game time. We were being booted out of the gym in the middle of our match to make way for their practice. And no one seemed to see anything wrong in that—no one but me. None of my arguments or curses changed the football team's plans, so we picked up our gear and stalked into the locker room. I fumed as I saw my girls experiencing the physical hurt that comes when an athlete has charged herself up for an athletic contest and then can't release that adrenalin in exercise.

But more insults were still to come. As we were halfway through our postgame showers, the Mira Costa football team started pounding on the door demanding the right to use the locker room at once. It is standard custom for the visiting men's teams to use the women's locker room, but this time it was obvious that no one bothered to check first to see if it would interfere with the women's schedule. Possibly no one cared. When the MCC footballers grew impatient, they sent in a couple of ogling volunteers to intimidate my women and force them to leave. My girls, who were still in the middle of their showers, were embarrassed by these characters. That was enough. I was in the middle of my shower, too, but I stormed out and marched dripping wet right up to the intruders. "Get the hell out of my locker room and I'll tell you when you can come back in!" I roared, waving a finger in their faces. Their jaws dropped and they retreated.

That was the first game of the season, and a good indication of the abuse my team and I would have to take. I was attempting to provide a legitimate athletic experience for my athletes, but I was met on all sides by the *recreational* emphasis other people wanted to put on women's sports. Another time my team had to play a completely unpracticed Arizona Western College team of twenty girls who had piled into a station wagon thinking they were going for a play day at the beach. This match was arranged by a man who seemed to be more concerned about the yacht cruise and barbecue after the games than he was about the legitimacy of the athletic contest. My team members looked at me in disbelief when they realized that they weren't going to get to challenge themselves and the new defense that we had just practiced that week because the other team couldn't even get the ball over the net. They were hurt; I was furious. Yet I was chastised for not making it mandatory for my team to attend the festivities that surrounded this farce. We had just experienced an insult to our athletic talent. I didn't blame my girls one bit when they weren't interested in socializing.

Many of the young women I coached had been taught by their parents to believe that athletic participation for women was an insignificant activity. Many times my athletes had to leave practice early or even miss games because they were told to cook dinner or babysit for their families. Male athletes would hardly be asked to give up their athletics to perform domestic chores. In fact, most men are considered to be doing their bit for the family by participating in athletics. It makes for a troubling double standard.

Such basic attitudes toward women athletes are one area of disrespect. Finances are another. At Cal Poly, for example, I received a budget of $900 for women's track and field from the Women's Recreation Association—that's right, *recreation*—while the men's track coach received $9000.

At that time, I didn't know enough to fight for more funding, so I decided to do my best to ensure that my girls at least had the best possible athletic experience for the money. Instead of scheduling six or seven meets and operating on a shoestring, I chose to plan four or five meets and do them right. Half the educational value of intercollegiate athletics for men has always been the experience of travel, the exposure to new people and places, and the chance to learn to be on their own in a hotel room in a new city. My girls put in the same hours and sweated as hard as the men, and I was determined to give them a comparable opportunity. Every time we went to a track meet, we left the night before, stayed in a nice motel, and went to a good restaurant. As I watched my girls enjoying themselves, I remembered my own college track career—sleeping on the gym floor before a track meet and dining on bag lunches. I knew I was giving my girls an important experience, one that helped them feel they were truly athletes and that gave them lessons that academic schooling couldn't teach. I wanted them to see that being an athlete could be exciting. I wanted them to know that there is a big world out there to explore, and I wanted to give them a head-start on it. The freedom I was teaching them—independence physically and mentally—wasn't always appreciated.

My own personal, never-dull lifestyle began to come under attack. I came to the university assuming that my private life was private, but various colleagues apparently thought that my salary entitled the school to own me day and night. Again, I believe I was attacked under the double standard: behavior that was considered normal and acceptable in a single man was viewed as scandalous for me. My sins included interracial dating. When the black student activities director and I walked into the gym to watch a wrestling match one night, several college administrators acted as if we were invisible. I left town each weekend to visit various men in other towns, and the grin on my face every Monday morning showed the good time I'd had.

Anyone well known or important who came to town ended up staying at the house in which I was living. When Senator Alan Cranston visited San Luis Obispo, he and his entourage came to visit for the evening. I had trained with him the year before in Washington (he competes in the master's division of the AAU). When Doc Ogilvie, the nationally known sports psychologist, spoke at Cal Poly, he also visited; I had been very close to him during my SJS days, when he was the "jock" counselor and confidant. Any Olympic athletes wandering between Los Angeles and the Bay Area used our place as a halfway rest spot, and our spontaneous parties made our house a hot spot in an otherwise quiet town.

One of the older faculty members sat me down one day for a heart-to-heart talk. She was a sweet, gray-haired woman who was regarded as the mother-figure of the department. "You know, Lynda, I really think it would be best for everyone concerned if you made sure your private life was kept completely out of view of the students," she told me. "You do lead quite a fast life—New York one weekend, L.A. and San Jose all the other weekends." The more I listened the angrier I became. "You've become quite an idol for these young women," she continued, "and I don't really think it would be fair to them to let them think they could live the same life that you do."

"Why not?" I thought. I'd struggled to achieve a lifestyle that combined a career and an active social life, and I certainly didn't agree that it would harm the students to know that becoming a physical education instructor did not necessarily mean that they had to live in a nunnery. I believed I was widening the p.e.-teacher stereotype and doing these future teachers a favor.

The Cal Poly p.e. department saw me as irresponsible and loose; I saw them as rigid and unimaginative. We were probably both right at one time or another, and probably our students learned from both approaches. But my tolerance wasn't shared by the department: a decision was made to reopen my position the following year, and the search began for my replacement. My favorable student evaluation wasn't enough to save my job.

I was learning that as a teacher I would have to struggle with the same pressure to conform that I had felt as an undergraduate. I saw a conflict between the old generation of women physical educators, many of whom have had no competitive athletic background, and the new generation of women athletes who have struggled to establish their own athletic identities (usually by turning to a man's world) and now wanted to develop drastically improved college athletic programs for women. The dilemma as I saw it was that the older women were tenured, while the younger ones were more competitive, more athletic, more ambitious but less in a position to implement change. The older women were well-qualified teachers of physical education, but not the coaches of highly trained athletes.

15

⇥≫ ≪⇤

The Oberlin Experience

"He read my mind," I thought when I first read Jack Scott's book *Athletics for Athletes* while I was a graduate student at San Jose State, before I started teaching. Scott showed me that I hadn't been so much a rebel as an athlete who was unwilling to sell out to the coaches' rule. Attitude problem? Uncoachable? All the criticisms that physical educators and coaches had leveled at me over the years suddenly became compliments. I was an athlete who wanted to have a say in what happened to her.

Scott's approach to athletics was a revelation. All the time that I had studied or participated in sport, I had no sense of how the sports establishment operated. I had no overview of my profession. Scott said that the powers that ruled athletics wanted me and all other athletes as naive as I to stay that way. While physical educators and sportswriters dealt in poetic generalities about the character-building "values" of athletic endeavor, Scott talked about the ugly reality. He analyzed the power structure that dominates athletes and showed how big business subverts sport for profit motives.

Long before Jack and Micki Scott hit the front pages of every newspaper in America for their alleged involvement in the Patty Hearst case, they were considered radicals. For some time Jack has been a voice opposing the domineering sports establishment. His and Micki's political views extend further to the left than mine, but much of what they would like to see changed in this country makes sense to me.

After my house was surrounded by visibly armed FBI agents while Micki and Jack were visiting me one night in the winter of 1975, they made their decision to go underground. For six weeks while they were underground, much of the media billed them as guilty parties in a conspiracy to harbor fugitives. If there is any truth to the charges I'm sure Micki and Jack would see it as a conspiracy to save lives. I, along with many of the Scotts' other friends across the country, was subjected to surveillance for several weeks after their disappearance. The people I phoned or visited during the next two weeks were visited by the FBI shortly after my contact with them. All of these incidents reinforced in my mind the "Big Brother" kinds of comments that Jack and Micki had made about the government. I had always felt that they had been paranoid before; now it was my turn to have reason to be paranoid.

Micki and Jack resurfaced at a San Francisco press conference in April where they dared the government to arrest or subpoena them if they had done anything wrong. Four months went by before the government issued subpoenas, yet for over 6 months the FBI had been harassing them and their friends. In addition to their ongoing work in sports, the Scotts are now speaking out about the grand jury system and FBI harassment. Jack and Micki are accustomed to taking a stand on controversial issues; up until this time, the main focus of their attention has always been sport.

Jack, a former Stanford sprinter, has advocated sport for sport's sake from the first time I had heard of him. He believes that athletic activity should be controlled by athletes and has even suggested the "radical" idea of using the democratic process to select coaches. Scott wants to see the end of tyrannical coaching and treatment of athletes as children. He wants a return to pure motives, to winning for the sake of excellence, not merely to fill the pockets of businessmen who own athletes.

Jack relates the financial perversion of modern sport to deeper problems in American society. He argues that sport, not religion, has become the opiate of the people, providing an outlet for the millions of workers herded into dehumanizing factory jobs. It was no coincidence, he has said, that big-time sport began at about the same time as the Industrial Revolution. The capitalists knew that their workers needed a release from the boredom and drudgery of their jobs, so they provided them with something that diverted them from active efforts to change their condition. Instead of organizing for a strike, workers joined the thousands brawling at a football game. In addition, big-time sport provided capitalists an opportunity for profit. The elite in the sports world became superstars, deliberate creations of the managers, both to fuel the fantasies of the common workers and to attract their hard-earned money.

I had always been thrilled by the glamour and excitement of football. I read in Jack's book that my heroes, the superstuds in their helmets and shoulderpads, were images conjured up by the moneymakers for profit. Behind the images were men who were ruthlessly controlled and relentlessly exploited by their owners.

Scott challenges the myths that sugarcoat sport in America. Many claim that violence on the playing field releases

Jack Scott, at left, meets with three of the coaches he hired soon after taking over as Oberlin athletic director: left to right, Tommie Smith, Cass Jackson, Pat Penn.

CREDIT: Micki McGee/ISSS

aggression that otherwise would lead to violence on the streets. Scott charges that the blood-lust spectacles of bigtime football or hockey could actually increase violence. Further, he argues, why are we looking for outlets for aggression when we should be trying to alleviate the causes of that aggression? The mythmakers say that sports teaches values—fair play, teamwork, play-to-win-but-play-by-therules. Scott asks who makes the rules. Who controls access to the game?

Scott believes that sports should be reformed from the ground up, and many of his ideas challenge the existing structure of high school and college athletics. He wants college athletes to have a voice in the selection of their coaches. He wants to break down traditional male–female barriers in sports education wherever possible. He wants sports education to be made relevant to students, and he thinks that expensive school facilities should be available to the entire community when not in use.

Scott's suggestions sounded good to me on paper and I learned that soon he would have a chance to try them out. The liberal new president of Oberlin College, Robert Fuller, had invited Scott to become the college's director of athletics. My interest in Scott's plans became more than academic when I heard that he had chosen Tommie Smith as track coach and assistant athletic director. Cass Jackson, former assistant coach at San Jose State, was signed on as head football coach. (Jackson was the first black to hold this position at a predominantly white college.) As head basketball coach, Scott hired Pat Penn, who the season before had led an Ohio high school basketball team to the state championship. Oberlin's top coaching staff was an all-black triumvirate.

Scott's personal choices set the sports world buzzing, but Oberlin seemed like the right place to embark on a radical experiment. The town of 9000 was about 40 percent black and boasted a proud history as a hotbed of abolitionist sentiment before the Civil War. Many slaves who had been smuggled north on the Underground Railroad found in Oberlin, just across the Ohio River, their first taste of freedom. Oberlin was also one of the first predominantly white male colleges to admit women and blacks.

Progressive educators who were familiar with Jack's books (his second was *The Athletic Revolution*) looked to Oberlin as a test of the radical sports movement. As it turned out, I was to view the Oberlin experience firsthand. A teaching post became vacant in the summer of 1973, and Tommie Smith and Cass Jackson recommended me for the job. Soon I was meeting the leading radicals of sport.

The Scotts were not at all what I expected. I had grown used to sports reformers on the order of Harry Edwards, who radiates excitement and energy in every direction. Jack surprised me with his mildness, his calm manner of moving and speaking. Jack folded his long sprinter's legs and sat crosslegged on the floor. I felt ridiculous in the dress I'd worn to meet my new employer. Obviously I wasn't dealing with the educational establishment. I kicked off my shoes and sat on the floor too.

Jack struck me as a composite—a professor's head on an athlete's body. A balding blond, he has a face dominated by extraordinarily inquisitive eyes. Light blue and piercing, Scott's eyes are always on the move. He rarely looks at any one person or thing for a long time; he's always seeking out, analyzing, reflecting, and moving on. To me, the man is brilliant. I was impressed by his intelligence the moment he spoke.

Micki came in to join us. Very slim, she was wearing a halter top and shorts, and I could tell that some time in her life she had done something athletic because she carried herself with strength and confidence. She was one of those mystery women. She seemed to glide in and out of a room without moving a particle of air. Until I came to know her, I thought she had some power of silent communication because I never seemed to hear her saying anything, yet things were always happening around her. Micki speaks quietly, carefully, intensely. I was used to the casual, flirtatious social energy I threw out everywhere I went. Micki was intense and dead serious.

Not that the Scotts didn't have a sense of fun. They certainly did. But their humor had an intellectual quality I'd never experienced before. They poked fun at politicians, the government, and powerful people in the establishment. Underlying everything they did was a strong sense of purpose.

Micki and Jack were always involved in a million projects. I was almost totally apolitical, but I could see that their lives were dedicated to the goal of freeing the masses from the rule of the exploitive few. Phone calls were always coming in or going out to Cesar Chavez, Dick Gregory, the media people they trusted (they didn't trust many), and countless athletes who needed support when they ran into conflicts with the sporting establishment. Posters of Chairman Mao, Martin Luther King, and Cesar Chavez hung on the walls, and exciting talk filled the room. The people who came to their house were activists; they had all written books, produced films, given lectures, worked in the farm worker movement or the sports revolution or in political organizing.

When Jack eventually resigned his Oberlin position, he was given his full three years' salary even though he worked only a year and a half. Most people envied the Scotts' windfall, but Micki told me that they gave most of that money to the Attica defense fund and other radical projects.

I have always been struck by the injustice of Micki's public image. "And his wife Micki" the press inevitably seems to say when writing of the Scotts. But the Scotts have come very close to establishing a one-to-one male–female relationship that doesn't force either of them into a leader or follower role. Jack can just as easily vacuum the rug while Micki makes an important phone call; they try to share all responsibilities. The Scotts' relationship involves a lot of giving and sharing, and both of them are the strength and activism that has been labeled Jack Scott.

Together they founded the Institute for the Study of Sport and Society, a nonprofit organization meant to examine the political, economic, and social implications of sport in America. The institute produced books such as Dave Meggyesy's *Out of Their League*, which criticizes pro football, and Gary Shaw's *Meat on the Hoof*, a critique of college football. In addition, Jack and Micki issued the monthly "ISSS Newsletter," an overview of current developments in sport with key items supplied by the Scotts' vast network of athlete friends. The newsletter tackled subjects the establishment either ignored or inadequately covered. It reported in detail on such stories as black athletes' fights to fire racist coaches, and George Sauer's decision to quit the New York Jets because of the inhumane treatment of football players. Often Jack and Micki invited their writers into their home; Meggyesy, for example, lived with them and talked his story while Jack wrote the book and Micki served as editor and photographer. Sport authors and theoreticians frequently appeared and added to the excitement of the Scott house.

My meeting with Jack and Micki made a tremendous impression on me. So, when an opening occurred on the Oberlin staff, I applied for the position. I liked the idea of working with Tommie and Cass, and the post appealed to me for professional reasons as well. I had all but given up hope of implementing a new approach to women's physical education with a traditional p.e. department. I was tired of being labeled the adolescent rebel who critics said would someday grow up and accept the real world. Scott offered me a chance to be in a power position for a change, and the change was more than welcome.

The power struggle surrounding my appointment should have told me that the Scotts had landed in a minefield at Oberlin. Although Jack, Cass, and Tommie wanted me for the job, the search for a new woman physical educator had to follow strict procedures. After a lengthy screening process, three finalists were selected, including me. The physical education department voted for me unanimously. Unfortunately the College Faculty Council, which also had to approve my appointment, suspected a Scott ploy. Unanimity was suspect in a department that had such strong pro-Scott and anti-Scott forces. Opposition to my appointment increased. I spent late summer packing my bags, then unpacking them, until Tommie called to tell me that a compromise had been reached: I was to share an assistant professor's position with Claudia Coville, the candidate of the conservative forces. After a lot of doubts on my part, and a lot of persuasion from Jack, I accepted the job.

The scene I saw when I arrived in Oberlin left me confused. I had expected to be part of a new program of growth and change. But that change had already begun and it had seriously upset the natives. My time in Oberlin was one of constant argument and power plays, and the prime losers were the Oberlin students.

A nasty display of racism convinced me from the first that Oberlin's pre-Civil War liberalism had disappeared. When I first arrived, Tommie took me to a boarding house next door to Jack and Micki's place to arrange for a room. I wasn't impressed by the place, but the price was right and I liked being near the Scotts. After I looked at the room, I told the woman I'd call her when I'd made my decision and walked out to Tommie, who was standing next to his golden Porsche. Together, Tommie and I drove off, and I saw that the woman's face had dropped to her knees. She hurried into the house and slammed the door.

Later that afternoon, I called her to say that I'd take the room and would bring her a check. She fumbled, stuttered, and finally blurted out, "No . . . no . . . I don't think . . . no . . . we really can't . . . I just can't have people like that coming through my house."

"People like that." Tommie was a world-record holder, an Olympic-gold-medal winner, and a faculty member at a leading college, but because he was black he couldn't come to that woman's cheap boarding house. After that incident, my opinion of Oberlin was pretty low, and subsequent events did nothing to improve it.

I stayed for a while at Cass Jackson's house—a move that had the local gossips buzzing—and spent much of my time at Jack and Micki's. The Scotts' home was an oasis. The Scotts operated an open house with a steady flow of friends moving in and out. (To some Oberlin eyes, the place was a commune, a bunch of hippies living together.) Among the visitors who added excitement to the central cast of ex-Californians were Del Martin, former Stanford sprinter and then instructor of sport and politics; Paul Hoch, sports theoretician; Dave Meggyesy and George Sauer Jr. Students were always welcome. The Scott cafeteria, as we called it, was open long after the town had closed up.

The weather was so bad in Oberlin that winter (it is the second most overcast county in the USA) that none of us bothered remembering if it was day or night; we had to stay in all the time anyway. Many nights the Scotts' front room jumped with intensity. Conversation and critiques of society went on long into the night and morning. When anyone got tired he or she would sleep. When there was something happening, we would stay up. Traditional life had been suspended as we all threw ourselves into this stimulating environment in the middle of Oberlin's conservatism. To all of us Californians, the weather was so severe that many nights we all slept right where we were when our energy faded and we neeeded rest, rather than venture out.

Jack and Micki were invaluable catalysts for my own thinking: Jack knew more about pro sport, and Micki seemed more knowledgeable about women's athletics—together they had an answer for every question. (Not that I accepted everything they said. For a long time I wondered whether all the complaints about pro football might not be just the griping of a couple of malcontents. Later, I came to agree with much of their criticism after becoming friendly with several Redskins and learning what they went through.) The Scott Front Room Crowd was patient with newcomers like me. They were used to dealing with athletes who hadn't ever thought about anything more complicated than their next competition. The Scotts talked of radical politics, of a reform of the entire government, and of sport, and I took it all in. I read the newspapers and magazines spread around the house and talked into the night with the Scotts' friends.

The Scotts' radical lifestyle and philosophy may have annoyed many of the Oberlin elite, but Jack's policies as athletic director of the college outraged them. Major and minor sports were always given such unequal emphasis in both the high schools and the colleges, but Jack wanted to see athletes in all sports receive equal recognition. He did away with entrance fees into the major sports such as football and basketball to help rid spectators of the feeling that, "If I'm paying $5 to see this, it must be good." Other sports such as wrestling and ice hockey had never charged, and many potential spectators assumed it was because there was really nothing to see. Jack believes that spectators tend to think that if they've paid to see an event, they are entitled to the kind of entertainment they personally want, rather than what the team gives. Jack didn't want to have to feel responsible to spectators who might not want to see a black coach or a Chicano quarterback.

Jack was militantly anti-elitist and didn't believe in the separation between town and gown that had prevailed at Oberlin. When he realized how little the Oberlin athletic facilities were used he decided to open the college's three basketball gyms, seven racquetball courts, seven squash courts, sauna, weight room, and swimming pool to the community.

Of course, certain privileged members of the Oberlin society were not happy with the change. The college athletic facilities had served as a country club for wealthy alumni and big businessmen. These men had their own private locker room in the multimillion dollar Phillips Gym. College staff members—except the buildings and grounds crew—were also allowed to use the gym and locker room.

"They kept out the building and grounds crew to keep out the blacks," Jack explained to me. "That had to change." Jack's decision to open the facilities to the community at certain hours caused hysteria among the alumni and staff. These white folks weren't used to seeing a lot of black kids playing in their gym. Jack's share-the-wealth philosophy benefited women students, too. Before he became athletic director, most women's activities were held in an old rickety gym. When women did come into the new gym, they had second-class status. For example, the equipment room was connected to the men's locker room; to check out a piece of equipment, women had to hang around a little square-foot window and hope to get someone's attention. The men's locker room also provided sole access to the sauna.

Jack decided to give the men's faculty locker room to the women. Next he put up curtains to allow privacy in the men's locker room but also to create a walkway for women to the equipment room and sauna. Jack's egalitarian moves infuriated most alumni and faculty. Now they had to take showers with the lowly students in the community men's locker room.

Scott was one of the few male athletic directors in the country who believed in women's sport. He tripled funding for women's athletic teams his first year at Oberlin, but money alone couldn't do the job. The tenured women professors at Oberlin were interested in traditional physical education, not in developing athletes. To defeat Jack, they borrowed a technique from veteran footdraggers in Congress. They established committees and subcommittees, had endless meetings, and never seemed to accomplish anything. Oberlin's women students had plenty of athletic talent, but at least two of their physical education instructors absolutely refused to coach, either because they knew they weren't qualified or because they did not believe in the concept of intercollegiate athletics for women. One woman faculty member actually stated that "no mature woman would want to play a physical team sport like basketball." Many sports were shortchanged. For example, instead of developing a systematic coaching program in swimming, a community woman was hired, a sociologist who could barely stay afloat, for $500 a season.

Even when the administration had an instructor interested in coaching—me, for example—they did their best to sabotage a competitive approach to athletics. Oberlin had a women's volleyball team with real potential, but it was coached by a faculty woman whose only acquaintance with the sport had been a coaching clinic the previous summer. The woman was well-meaning, but she didn't have a basic understanding of the game. I had had plenty of experience in volleyball and asked to take over. Instead, the women's athletic establishment assigned me to coach basketball, a sport I didn't feel qualified to handle. I cringed at the thought. Coaching basketball was a humiliating experience for me. I was used to the feeling of control that comes only with knowledge and experience, but as basketball coach, I never had the assurance I could give anything to my athletes.

While battles raged in the activities classes, Jack's new academic offerings also outraged some faculty members. The physical education curriculum was now sparked with such courses as Sport and Society, Women in Sport, Sport Literature, and Sport and Politics. Jack wanted to smash the "dumb jock" stereotype that has crippled p.e. for so long and to develop a new generation of athletes capable of independent thought and analysis.

Jack took his democracy seriously and gave students parity in the decision-making process. An elected student representative had an equal vote with every faculty member at departmental meetings. Athletes were allowed to have a vote in the screening process for coaches. The year before I came, the football players had elected Cass Jackson coach, a decision that sent several long-time Oberlin athletic faculty members scurrying to more conservative havens. (They followed a previous exodus of faculty members who fled when Jack and Tommie were hired.) Jack and his supporters believed that students, faculty, and coaches should work together to form the most relevant education possible. The anti-Scott forces argued that students weren't knowledgeable enough to determine their academic or coaching needs. After Cass Jackson's election, yet another struggle began as faculty moved swiftly to take away the athlete's vote.

Even the Ohio Athletic Conference had its problems with the new Oberlin. When the men's cross country team held a home meet and Oberlin's women had no event that day, the cross country coach invited the women into the meet on a strictly exhibition status. Apparently some of the non-Oberlin coaches were unhappy about their runners racing against women, and one coach filed a protest with the OAC. When the OAC held a conference meeting to condemn Oberlin's policy of integrating the sexes in sport, the Scott faction picketed—a Berkeley-like move that confused and frightened those conservative midwesterners.

The Scott experiment at Oberlin was short-lived. President Fuller announced his resignation during a policy battle in the fall of 1973 and suddenly the heat was on Jack. The Educational Planning and Policies Committee (EPPC) launched a thorough investigation of the physical education department in an effort to discredit Jack's program. Then it announced that Scott's job would be divided, that the athletic director could not be chairman of the Physical Education Department. The committee also recommended returning the curriculum to the traditional format. Scientific courses in anatomy, physiology, and kinesiology were again to be emphasized, and Scott's political and social analysis courses were to be eliminated.

Obviously Scott could not tolerate such a direct challenge to his leadership. He even was told that he, Cass, or Tommie would have to go the following year. Tommie and Cass were both up for evaluation and possible renewal of their contracts, so Jack was the only one of the three who didn't have to fear for his job the following year. Yet he was presented with an offer. If he would leave, just go quietly, the college would pay him his full three-year salary after having worked only a year and a half. He considered the alternatives. He could stay and probably see Cass or Tommie left jobless the following year; or he could take their offer with a promise that both Tommie's and Cass's contracts would be renewed. Once it was guaranteed in writing that Tommie and Cass were hired for another three-year period Jack resigned at the end of January. Shortly thereafter eleven other administrative and faculty members hired by Fuller also left Oberlin.

After Jack's resignation, the conservative element did its best to return Oberlin to "normal." By the end of the next semester, student parity in departmental decision making was eliminated. A department chairman more sympathetic to the administration was appointed, and the department began its return to its safe, traditional approach to physical education.

Jack's ideas might have seemed completely reasonable in a Berkeley environment, but when moved to Oberlin, Ohio, they confronted incredible opposition. Jack's policies, class offerings, and approach to physical education were innovative and creative. They could cause positive change in sport and physical education if implemented and supported properly. The shame of the entire Oberlin experiment is that many watchful physical educators across the country now feel that his theories have proved unrealistic. To the contrary, I believe the circumstances and the personnel involved were the true cause of the failure.

16

→≫ ≪←

Looking at Sport Through Oberlin Eyes

I left Oberlin's teaching staff shortly after Jack Scott resigned. My decision was one of the hardest I've ever made. I was fascinated by the new Oberlin the Scotts had tried to create and wanted to help carry on their work, but I was weary of the continual battling between conservatives and reformers. My shared appointment with Claudia Coville was pure havoc. The split in authority and responsibility meant that we continually interfered with one another, and our students were the losers. I felt I was being exploited by the college—I worked full-time for a half-time salary. When the college dragged its heels on my request for full-time status, I left.

But the Scotts' Oberlin never left me. I never again saw sport with the same eyes. All my life I had been a believer in the rah-rah athletic scene. Now I was finding flaws in what I had seen as so perfect. I wanted to see athletics that were for the athlete. I wanted to see sport oriented toward the participant, not the spectator, or worse, the entrepreneur who sells the tickets. I wanted athletes to learn to fulfill themselves in peak moments of physical and mental unity, not destroy their bodies to provide a moment's spectacle and then be cast away. I realized that all sports were male-identified and that I had developed that male orientation. Now I wanted to see women strike out and make sport their own. I no longer worried that some thought the Scotts and their friends were mere malcontents. I looked at my own experience and saw that there was a lot of truth in what they said.

Football is the best example of what's gone wrong with sport in America, and my worshipful reaction to it exemplified the feelings that the media creates. At Oberlin I talked with George Sauer Jr., a man quietly bitter because of the football establishment's unwillingness to treat him as a man. Meeting Dave Meggyesy caused me to rethink the myths of true valor promoted by the football propagandists. Perhaps a man who played with pain wasn't just a true champion; perhaps he was also the victim of an owner or coach who sees his athletes as meat useful only to better balance the financial sheets.

In the summer of 1974 I had a chance to see for myself close-up the truth of George and Dave's theories. The National Football League's Player's Association had called a strike of its members and the Washington Redskin veterans worked out at Georgetown University on their own until the strike was called off and they went back to camp. Georgetown was my home track whenever I worked out in Washington, so it was inevitable that I would get involved. One sweaty afternoon I ran into George Starke, offensive tackle of the Redskins. As I talked with George, another member of the team zoomed in on me. "Hey baby, I *know* you lift weights with legs like that," he said. "Can I just touch one of 'em?"

"Sure, knock yourself out," I answered, not to be intimidated. It amused me that these men, whose muscles are their meal ticket, seldom have contact with athletic women or strong muscular female bodies. It also amuses me that so many athletes come on with women by attempting to intimidate them.

Once I retaliated, meeting these players with my own version of physical intimidation, we were able to relax and relate to one another. These characters reminded me of the Speed City Gang—men with cocky sureness and pride in their physical accomplishments. I felt right at home.

After one particularly satisfying and exhausting workout together, wide receiver Frank Grant and I were walking toward the locker room. We were enjoying the athletes' natural high. The fans, gathered to watch the Redskins practice, soon brought us down. Some kids approached Frank and without knowing who he was asked for autographs. "Why do you want my autograph?" he asked them. "Well you're a Redskin, aren't ya'?" one answered. That was reason enough for him. "Get her autograph," said Frank, motioning toward me and winking. "She's a track star." "Nah," the little boy answered, "she's one of the Redskins' wives." Already that boy knew that only Redskins counted in the world and that women weren't athletic. (The boy also knew immediately that I couldn't be married to this particular Redskin. Frank is black.) I spent the rest of the summer learning a lot about the pro football player's mentality and lifestyle.

Unlike track athletes who *can* baby their bodies, football players can't complain about their hurts. However, as an athlete, I could see what they went through. At a December 1974 game in Los Angeles, Redskin wide receiver Roy Jefferson played with a chronic pulled quadracep muscle. Instead of sitting out the game as his body screamed he should, the team physician shot him full of pain-killers when the game started and he played with a deadened upper thigh. When the Xylocaine wore off, Frank Grant, his backup, played until half time, when Roy was shot up again and "ready" to play the third quarter. Mike Bass, a cornerback, played that same game with two cracked ribs and a disclocated shoulder—again, pain-killers made it possible.

Patty Van Wolvelaere watched the game with me. We were amazed at the abuse these men heaped on their bodies. Patty was having Achilles tendon trouble at the time and had passed up several meets to allow time for recuperation. I had a foot injury and had resigned myself to a month of swimming instead of running. I had to take the strain off that foot long enough for it to heal properly. Patty and I looked at the Redskin scene and couldn't believe it: how can an athlete play well when he's injured? And isn't a muscle that's injured and numbed likely to be damaged permanently in the heat of the game?

There is a marked difference between that almost pleasurable physiological pain that is sought in a day's workout and the pain that tells you you just can't continue. Perhaps one day your body is feeling sharp. Maybe your wind is so good you feel that you could run forever. But a sharp pain develops in a tendon next to the ankle or just below the knee. Your body is saying stop. The various tendons that connect our muscle structure to our bones don't have the same elasticity or resiliency as the soft tissues. When something is wrong with a joint, a tendon, or a bone, it needs rest. Further stress simply increases the possibility of permanent injury. A track athlete must learn to differentiate between good and bad pain—a potential injury versus the normal aches and pains that plague anyone who is vigorously active. Football players and other pros in big money sports are not allowed to listen to their own bodies.

Surprisingly, my Redskin friends defended the play-with-pain ethic. "A good pro athlete can play at 85 percent efficiency and still benefit his team," Jefferson claimed. "Besides," Bass said, "the teamwork is highly sophisticated, especially on defense. When I'm not there, Chris Hanburger's linebacking job changes because he's used to what I can and can't do, and anyone else in my slot will play differently."

I listened to them rationalize and still wasn't convinced. "Don't you feel like a piece of meat playing when you're all bruised up like that?" I persisted.

"Not much of one," Frank answered. "I don't feel like anything. I just crawl home and lick my wounds." Frank is almost continually jiving, but I wasn't completely sure he was jiving this time. In order to play the game, pro players have to believe they have everything under control. They would never admit that their bodies were being used by the meat market of pro football.

Pain-killers aren't the only drugs used to beef up athletes' bodies. Anabolic steroids are taken to increase muscle mass and add weight. These drugs are made from male hormones and actually usurp the work of the testicles in the male, causing shrinkage and sometimes impotency during the time of steroid ingestion; yet they are taken by many linemen in football and by weight-event athletes including weight lifters, shot-putters, and discus throwers. The pressure to take these drugs, which distort the body's true capability, is almost impossible to resist. Even women have gotten into the act. I know one woman shot-putter, a purist, who for years refused to take steroids until she realized that it was impossible for an undrugged body to compete in a field of drugged ones.

Amphetamines, or uppers, are another drug widely used in athletics. I saw their effect on the athletes' minds and bodies that summer with the Redskins. The Football Players' Association strike ended unsuccessfully, and the players agreed to report to camp on a Tuesday evening. I saw many of the 'Skins the Monday before they left, and they were the same easygoing, fun guys I'd worked out with all month.

Four days later I met several of them after an exhibition game against Buffalo. They had completely changed. Where had my buddies gone? Who were these walking zombies? A lineman grabbed me by the neck and physically threatened me if I didn't go back to his room with him for the night. These guys were cranked up and wired up and didn't even begin to have that natural physical high I knew after track meets. They were *up*, but they were also *used up*. They had scratches and holes where skin should have been and they looked like they had been in a street brawl. Strangely, my player friends didn't realize that they were different people. In four short days the coaches had brutalized them. Now they were mentally ready for pro football; now they had their "game heads" together.

Later that year when I told Redskin George Starke what I had seen, he answered, "Were we gone only four days? That trip to camp felt like a month."

After Scott Front Room conversations, I saw that many pro athletes accept these taxing working conditions because they have little choice. Sport is a large portion of their identity; many of these guys haven't learned to do anything else. College educations for pro athletes are generally a farce; colleges often serve in effect as cheap farm teams for pro clubs.

I looked back at my experience at San Jose State. Many of its "college" athletes simply weren't college material intellectually. SJS, like most other colleges, had a 2 percent plan—2 percent of the student body were admitted even though they did not meet the college's academic standards. The men's athletic teams used up almost all the 2 percent slots, although an occasional music or drama student slipped in on the same plan. The effect of this "generous" plan was to allow minority students from deprived educational backgrounds to attend SJS, donating their athletic services to the college.

Each semester athletes registered for courses ahead of the

other students. Theoretically, they went first so that they could register for classes that didn't conflict with practice. A side benefit was that all the easy (and useless) courses were still open. The coaches didn't want their athletes to enroll in courses that would be too difficult. After all, they might fail them and become ineligible for the team.

I must have written more than a dozen papers for athletes who would have been ruled ineligible were it not for me. At the time I felt like Florence Nightingale saving her dying men from the sword of the enemy. But did I really do my friends a favor? My ghostwriting service might have been worthwhile if an athlete needed help in a one-shot, save-a-life situation. But most of these "students" never did any of their work themselves. They found some campus chickie or secretary who helped them out for a kiss on the cheek. I thought I was a buddy when I did their work. Only after the Scotts showed me how college sports uses young athletes did I realize I had helped perpetuate an exploitative system.

Many of my athlete friends ended up sadly. Thanks to their coaches and people like me, they were kept eligible to compete in sport for four years, but when the four years of eligibility were over, so was their schooling. Most lacked the money to continue on their own, so they failed to graduate. The luckiest ones were signed up by the pros, but even they had an uncertain future. One of the hottest SJS football players was a high draft choice of the St. Louis Cardinals, but he was injured during his senior year. Despite an operation, his knee never regained full motion and he was never able to play again. Since he had not prepared an alternate career—and none of his academic counselors took better care of his future than he did—he was left on his own to attempt to obtain a degree and a job. Another ex-SJS friend, an internationally known track star, was kept eligible through several years of college while reading at third-grade level. The last I heard he was bouncing around between Los Angeles and Philadelphia trying to hustle a living.

All through college these men were superstars. They were encouraged to focus their lives on a moment's glory and forget the future. After college, white athletes are often helped by prosperous alumni who find them jobs; but black athletes usually have no one in their corner. A world-caliber sprinter and close friend of mine, now unemployed says he has nothing to show but medals and trophies, and he now regrets that he lost his chance for a degree. "Yeah," he says, "you got your M.A. all right, and I got my M.F."

Many college athletes who graduate to the pros feel that sport is their only chance of "making it." Athletic eminence guarantees a job and status; without it you're broke and nobody. For example, sports stardom allows many black athletes to escape "nigger" status in our society; Chris Fletcher of the San Diego Chargers had a hard time buying a house in San Diego until the label Charger was put next to his name. "I wasn't black anymore," he told me in disgust.

Once, New York City cops broke in on George Starke and me with guns drawn. They thought they were confronting burglars, and they lowered their guns only because I stepped forward into the light of their flashlights and was recognized as an inhabitant of the apartment. Had George stepped into their view instead, their extremely nervous state could well have resulted in gunfire. George, normally known as a big football hero, would have just been a big "nigger" and therefore another police statistic.

Many fans can't believe that athletes are exploited by coaches and owners because of the big-money myths that surround pro sport. True, there are a few sports millionaires. But the average NFL player makes about $35,000 a year. That figure sounds high until you realize that the average career of a running back is four to five years; the lineman averages ten or eleven years. A permanent injury can make that kind of money seem like a very bad bargain, and even the pro who makes it out of the game intact can have a hard time supporting himself, let alone continue to pay the big bills of the high life he's learned to love.

Many players accept these conditions because they're hooked on the fantasy, the superstar image, and the adulation of the fans—intangible but very real commodities. But brutality seems quite a high price to pay.

Who ingrains brutality into these men? Much of the blame must be laid on tyrannical coaches who rule athletes with an almost military domination. Athletes are rarely allowed to exercise their own judgment. Norm Van Brocklin, former Atlanta Falcons coach, was notorious for stepping into his athletes' lives and governing their appearance. Players couldn't have sideburns, white laces in their shoes, or unusual taping around their wrists. Any personal flourish during a game was ruled out. Even in their personal lives, Atlanta Falcons were not to be seen in bellbottoms. "If they want to wear bellbottoms, they can join the navy," Van Brocklin was reported to have said. Evidently he figured his way of dressing and living was the standard everyone had to imitate.

Basically the coaches aren't granting their athletes credit as real human beings with independent lives and the ability to make adult decisions. When a player thinks like an adult, acts like an adult and speaks out for his rights and the rights of his teammates, he is usually labeled a discipline problem, a rebel. That was the case with Roy Jefferson. When he was playing for Pittsburgh, he says, he felt a constant pressure from coaches and management to conform. He said the harrassment was subtle but constant. He was continually being fined arbitrarily for little infractions that other players got away with. The coaches used fines as a way to muzzle his independent mind and quick tongue.

Roy bitterly remembers a practice session when he was with the Pittsburgh Steelers. All but two of the wide receivers on the team were sidelined for various minor injuries. Roy was one of the injured. Only two rookies, who were trying to impress the coaches and earn themselves a job, were left doing the passing drills. Roy watched the action and realized that these two rookies were going all out on every play, something that he as an established veteran would not have done in that 92 degree, humid weather. But these rookies felt the pressure to run all out through the entire pass pattern on each play. Because there were only two of them, they were barely dragging themselves back to the line of scrimmage before it was their turn again.

The drill was to continue for forty-five minutes. Roy saw the exhaustion creeping in on these rookies and took it upon himself as a concerned human being to say something to the coach in charge of the drill. "Naturally," Roy told me later, "the coach treated me like a child, as if my thoughts were totally useless. As the drill progressed I got angrier. Those rookies were obviously overworking themselves, but would not have dared to stop for fear of immediate censure from the coaching staff. I pointed out the situation to another of the coaches, but was ignored again. When I went into the locker room after practice that day and saw the trainers carry one of those dudes in on a stretcher, I got furious. He was black, but he was turning all sorts of purples and dark blues. He was sweating so profusely drops were bouncing off of him as he went by. They actually had to pack his body in ice and take him to the hospital that day to save his life . . . I mean, the cat almost *died!* I packed my bag and left. I was so angry I knew I couldn't talk to anyone right then without letting my anger and my fists fly, so I just left. When I went back to camp the following day I found that particular coach and told him that until that day I had felt a real respect for him as a man and as a coach. But I could no longer feel that way. 'You nearly killed a man out there yesterday, and it wasn't because you didn't know what was happening. I pointed it out to you, yet you chose to ignore it and push a man whom you knew would do anything you asked beyond his own physical limits.' "

Roy continued his story. "I was fined for leaving camp, and was brushed off with the same kind of indifference that a parent would give a complaining child. Two weeks later I was traded. I was a discipline problem."

In fact, Roy was just reacting to a situation like an adult. He has a reputation as being an outspoken man, and as a result, he has always been labeled a rebel.

Too many coaches refuse to learn anything new from the athletes or to respect their minds and bodies. This failure to include the athletes' point of view occurs in less commercialized sports too. Yet a thinking athlete usually knows more about his or her own body than any coach. The coach has scientific and technical knowledge, but the athlete knows his own body's unique reactions and movement patterns. The natural character of each athlete's style must be allowed to develop. Individuality should not be stifled by some coach's rigid idea of good form.

Each athlete is also different psychologically. I personally respond to encouragement or mild criticism. Others rise to their best performance after a coach's anger has struck them. Yet some coaches have the same manner with all their athletes and feel that any one on the team must accept whatever treatment the coach hands out.

Typical of this species is a man I will call Brown, former head coach of a prominent track club in the East. Granted, the man has turned out some magnificent track athletes, but he has also broken several potentially good careers with his rigid coaching. I was on Brown's team for four months, but I never felt I belonged. Maybe I was an outsider because I was the only white sprinter, or because I wasn't virtually assured an Olympic berth like most of his sprinters. For whatever reasons, Brown never made me feel included, nor did he offer me the individual training program I needed.

As I got to know the other athletes on his team, I became convinced that their unwavering obedience to Brown was based on fear, rather than just admiration. Physically Brown wasn't much bigger than average size, but he was an incredibly forceful presence who kept his athletes in a state of terror. From the moment we arrived at a workout, my fellow athletes worried, "Where's Brown? What kind of mood is he in? Did he speak to you yet today?" Brown could be a million miles away and one of his runners who had lost a race would say, "Oh, I don't want Brown to find out I got beat." (Interestingly, Brown's athletes often turned in poor performances when away from the master.)

For a while I was a victim of the Brown spell and believed in *CoachGod.* I was so overwhelmed by him that he became my guru. I was awed by the man and wanted to do everything I could to please him. But that turned out to be the problem—I was running to please *him.* He had such psychological domination over us that we were all dependent on his approval for our feeling of self-worth.

Bill, a quarter-miler on the team, became one of Brown's statistics. Bill clearly had the talent to be a top runner, but Brown managed to undermine his confidence so badly that he never realized his full potential. When Bill missed a track meet because of the flu, Brown threw him off the team. Bill took over a year to recover from the loss, and he still feels that he needs Brown to do a proper workout. This otherwise strong-minded law student never learned to be independent and have confidence in himself as an athlete.

Brown had such mental control over me that I paid attention to him instead of my own body and was injured as a result. One day doing starts, I felt a twinge in my left quadracep muscle—an indication that I had already pushed it too far. Brown's workouts were much tougher than anything I'd endured at SJS. Five 220s was a Bud Winter workout, but Brown often demanded twenty-four. Then as the sun set, he'd take us into the gym to practice starts. Sympathy wasn't in Brown's makeup. When I mentioned my strained muscle, he was unimpressed.

"You get back in there and finish your starts," he yelled.

"But something's wrong."

"Put your butt in the blocks and finish." he said.

Two days later at a track meet, I pulled that muscle.

One day Brown ignored me after I failed to qualify for the finals in a 60-yard dash. My time hadn't been bad and I'd just recovered from that muscle pull, so I thought I'd done decently. Brown, however, talks only to winners, and when my guru turned his back on me as punishment, I was crushed. At last I realized that Brown's control of my mind was intolerable. There I was, twenty-four years old and a college professor, hiding in a dark corridor, miserable because my coach wouldn't talk to me. I saw that the priorities in my life had been distorted. I had always loved track, win or lose. Before Brown I found joy in competition and in the sense that I was exerting myself to the utmost. Now I was running to please a coach, not myself. Brown made sport into a win or get-out situation. I got out.

The belief that athletes are infants rather than adults is all too common. Many coaches are dishonest with their athletes. The lies start with recruiting, when college athletes are promised jobs, housing, cars, and money that often don't materialize once they are safely enrolled in the school. Money inducements are illegal at the college level, but many athletes I knew were promised cash payments anyway. When they asked the coach to pay up, the athletic department would point piously to the rules and say that the athlete must have misunderstood. Looking back on my role in recruiting, I see that I was an unwitting participant in this exploitative system. Various coaches would call me when they had a group of recruits coming to the campus and have me join them for dinner. Knowing my "I can and will do anything" attitude, they must have known that to use me as an example of the women on the SJS campus would help make a recruit opt for San Jose.

Other than recruiting lies, many coaches will stretch the truth about their athletes' performances. False times may be given in windsprints or time trials. Sometimes, the coach hopes to build confidence. But coaches also distort the facts about a performance in order to maintain psychological control over the athlete. The falsehoods also indicate the coaches' basic failure to respect athletes.

Many athletes know what it is to be treated like slaves by their coaches, but blacks and women face special prejudices. Racism is common, even in predominantly black sports such as track. On the SJS track, where life was fairly egalitarian, many black athletes felt they weren't recognized as individuals.

"Hell, I'm just horse number three," complained Ronnie Ray Smith, an Olympic 400-meter relay member. The coach had just called him by another sprinter's name. "Yeah, we all look alike" Ronnie added. "On the track I'm one hell of a fast nigger. But take me off the track and I'm just a nigger."

For years, UCLA's track coach, Jim Bush, wouldn't allow women to set foot on *his* track during prime-time workout hours. Even Jan Svendsen, while a UCLA student, wasn't allowed to use the shot-put circle (well away from the track) until 5:30. She was told she was a "distraction," a standard excuse to exclude women. The first day or so, the presence of women can distract male athletes who have grown accustomed to the sex segregation of the American sports scene. But the newness wears off, especially when the women know what they're doing.

But even when they're allowed to be part of an athletic scene, women often are made to feel uncomfortable. Many young women athletes have told me that they wouldn't work out in the weight room when it was filled with men

A typical weight room workout, this one at UCLA.

CREDITS: Micki McGee/ISSS

because of the pressure they felt. I first started working out in the SJS weight room on rainy days as a substitute for my running workouts. I had my "big brothers" from the track with me, so I was comfortable. Since then, though, I have picked up many strange vibrations when I'm the only female in that traditional male sanctuary. Federal City College has two universal gyms in its weight room. I've seen several male lifters switch from the one I'm using to the other one—as if they can't use the same machines I do. The Georgetown University weight room is quite small and has only one universal gym. My track buddy Bill has worked out there for years and tells me the reaction that he sees as I enter the room.

"First of all," Bill explains, "you catch everyone completely off guard as you stroll in, acting as if you belong there. But you *do* belong there—it's obvious as they watch you work out. Yet they can't quite believe that you would intrude in their all-male domain. If we're working out together, and I ask you for advice on a particular exercise or about an injury, they can't believe it. They assume that the only way I would be speaking to you would be either patronizingly or flirtatiously. The anxiety level in the room builds the minute you walk in. If Joe Georgetown was lifting 90 pounds on his bench presses and sees you doing the same, he immediately increases his poundage to 130, even if it kills him. Even though you aren't paying any attention to those other clowns, I sense their insides tightening up as they watch you go smoothly through your weight training program. All the while you're acting as if nothing the least bit unusual is happening, even though they're freaking behind this strange creature in the weight room."

This strange creature also had to fight for acceptance at Cowell's Beach in Santa Cruz, the hot spot of beach volleyball in northern California. For over three years I was made to feel like a weirdo, but I never really knew why. I would show up as early as possible to try to sneak onto the court for a few games before the crowd got there. Only two other women occasionally played on this beach, but they had volleyball-playing husbands—automatic partners. (The indoor game of volleyball is normally played with six players; the outdoor beach game usually consists of only two—the game is called "doubles".) For me to come up with a partner was always a minor miracle in those early breakthrough days. Even though I was as good a player as many of the intermediate men who played there, few guys wanted to play with a female. The men had come to play volleyball; the women, except for me, had all come to be with the men. Not that I wasn't attracted to those pretty tanned bodies on the courts; I was. But once I asserted myself not as an awed spectator but as someone who wanted part of the action, many of these men reacted negatively. To counteract that rejected "jock" feeling I would sometimes bring male friends with me. That further upset the status quo. A guy watching a girl play volleyball? Unheard of. And most of the men I brought with me couldn't stand the strain on their egos. They too assumed that men were supposed to be the doers while the women watched contentedly.

Segregation in sport, psychological domination by coaches, exploitation of athletes—these insights came directly out of my Oberlin experience. Today more athletes are arriving at a new level of awareness. They're no longer willing to believe in myths or to become myths. They're demanding their rights to become individuals and athletes.

17

→»» «««

Happy, Healthy, and Horny

I first realized that I might be a sexual object at the age of twelve, when I babysat in a house filled with *Playboys*. Before my curiosity had run its course that night I had taken some Saran Wrap and made myself a see-through blouse just like the ones worn by *Playboy* pinups. The results were disappointing—I had absolutely no need for a bra—but I found it exciting to think of myself in the same terms as those women in the magazine.

Fortunately, late bloomer that I was, I didn't tie my concept of self-worth to my mammary development. I was the only one in my eighth-grade class who didn't wear a bra, that symbol of becoming a woman. My mom bought me a trainer bra so I wouldn't feel left out when we changed our clothes in gym class, but I always sneaked into the bathroom first chance I had after I reached school and yanked the uncomfortable thing off. Who needed a bra to be somebody? I knew I could prove my importance on the basketball court or the trampoline. Eventually in high school I succumbed to the pressure to wear one of those nasty things. I didn't need it; I don't wear a bra now most of the time.

My cheerleader status in high school allowed me to bloom socially, and, for the first of many times, I found myself battering against the passive female stereotype. I had complete access to the big shots on campus, and I guess I was like a kid let loose in a candy store. I never intended to hurt anyone's feelings; I just wanted to act out mine. And mine, like any teenager's, were liable to change.

Number 44 caught two touchdown passes to win a game, and he was high on my "want list." But the list should have been posted from day to day to keep everybody up to date on my current favorite. Long before football season ended, I had half the eligible male population of Leigh High School furious with me. I couldn't understand them. Hadn't I always been truthful? I always let a guy know when I was crazy about him, and I always let him know when I was no longer spellbound. I might change my mind twice a day, but that was no reason to call me insincere, was it?

Didn't the star quarterback go out with a different girl every weekend? I hated the way most girls sat around waiting for Prince Charmings to call. I had become somebody in my own right—a cheerleader superstar—and I didn't want to be relegated to the role of some boy's girlfriend. According to the rules of the game, I was supposed to be a weak and submissive female, but that didn't fit into my plans.

Despite my reputation, I was almost totally ignorant about sex. Dirty stories bewildered me, then became a source of education. "Santa Claus came down the chimney and was met by a gorgeous, sexy, young thing with no clothes on. She asked if he could stay for a while. He said, 'Ho, ho, ho, I can't get up the chimney *this* way.' "

"What way?" I asked.

"There occurs in the sexually excited male, an erection of the organ which would no doubt prevent Santa Claus from rising back up the chimney," said the note one of my friends slipped me in English class.

Oh, yeah?, I thought. So that's how it all works.

One day in my junior year, my mother handed me a book that explained the location and function of all the male and female reproductive organs. This was my only formal lesson about the birds and the bees. My parents never discussed the practical realities of sex, just the rules. And there were plenty of rules. As my diary records, I believed those rules, and the least infringement sent me into a paroxysm of shame.

July 17, 1964

For the first time in my life I got high—real high. Jim, Gary, and I were at Gary's house. When his parents left, we went to get some 7 Up and then mixed some drinks. I chugged down quite a bit of vodka and whiskey and brandy; then we started to play strip poker. When we got to the underwear I pretended to be drunk and went out to swim, but then I didn't have to pretend anymore, because I was OUT-OF-IT! Jim really took advantage of the situation—he was all over me, but I was so high that I didn't really seem to care.

July 18, 1964

When I woke up this morning, I felt so guilty about last night. Jim and I almost went as far in one night as George and I did in a whole year. I think Jim called, but I wasn't home. I hope he doesn't tell and that we can still be as good friends as we were before. I hope he doesn't think anything TOO bad about me.

July 19, 1964

I'm really mad at Jim. Gary told me that Jim wasn't drunk at all, but knew what he was doing the whole time. When he went back to Gary's after taking me home, he told Gary that he had fun. I'm so mad. I talked to Gary a long time. He said that I just wasn't Lynda Huey that night. Whenever I think of what happened I get sick. Jim was really "pinged up" and if I hadn't resisted everything, he wouldn't have stopped, I'm sure.

July 20, 1964

I really feel horrible. Jim and I used to be such good friends and now there's a terrible barrier between us. My estimation of him has gone down so much. To think how much he took advantage really makes me mad. But yet I just can't hate him—we've had too much fun together. Funny how one little incident can wreck a friendship of three years. Maybe after it cools off we'll be able to talk again, but right now I feel as if I *have* to show him I won't put up with jazz like that.

That slip tormented me for the next year. I knew that if the story were spread around school, Jim would gain prestige, but I'd face complete disaster.

In college I began to meet people who didn't share my sexual fears and taboos. Many of my friends were proud of their vigorous sex lives, and these friends didn't seem evil to me—they were merely using a different rule book. I became curious, but I was still too afraid to act. I *knew* that guilt would ruin my life if I pushed myself to go too far. It must have seemed an eternity to First Lover before I could guiltlessly take *the* giant step. But First Lover convinced me that all would be well; or, rather, I convinced myself. I was in love, you know. Sex rationalized, I took the plunge:

February 6, 1967

CROSS OUT THE BIG "V" ON MY FOREHEAD!!!!

But First Lover had other lovers. Hurt when I found that out, I retaliated by spending the night with First Lover's roommate. When First Lover found out where I'd been he announced that "as far as I'm concerned you've just gone to the moon"—and I had my first introduction to the double standard among liberated men.

But at least I had gotten rid of those sexual fears that had engulfed me as a young girl. Gradually I allowed myself to join in my friends' sexually free lifestyle and found I enjoyed it.

I've always been a rebel, so it seems natural to me that I preferred the male angle on life. The men in any social situation were bolder and made all the moves. Most of my men were track athletes who acted as if I should jump at their every command and desire their world-record track bodies more than I loved life. They assumed that once a young thing was privileged to know such divinity, she would be hooked forever, unable to touch another man. But I heard so much of that overpowering male sexual arrogance in the gyms and on the track that I soon learned to deal with my own sexuality on the same terms. What was good for them was going to be good for me.

"You can't brag that you finally got over with *me*," I'd tell them, "because I finally managed to get next to *you*." It seemed right to fight fire with fire. I'd been around these guys long enough to hear their locker room talk and listen to them scheme; I saw how their minds worked when they thought of sex. Women were supposed to fall automatically in love the minute they had any sexual contact with a man. Men were insincere, but women didn't find out until after the moment of conquest, when they were left as the victims. I wasn't going to be one of their pushover chicks. I knew too well their attitude and knew I wanted no part of the traditional female sit-home-and-mope-over-your-man role. I was going to move with the best of them.

Nice resolutions, but twenty-one years of puritanical upbringing kept cramping my style. Those damn TV shows and movies undercut my morale with their endless streams of women finally fulfilled after finding true love. They promised women a Prince Charming. So I often decided that I *must* be in love, at least a little, if I could spend more than one night with someone. Inevitably I wound up believing something that wasn't true; I put men on pedestals I manufactured for them.

Obviously, this attitude made me vulnerable. I would find myself involved in a "normal" one-to-one emotional, sexual relationship, only to discover that I was forced to give up too much of myself to maintain it.

December 23, 1968

Everything between us was so strong this morning, but then when I left, I realized that I felt FREE away from him. Claustrophobia setting in.

February 26, 1969

Got up in time to go to class, but Bill didn't want me to go and wouldn't take me, so I got pissed and just LEFT. It took me over two hours in class just to get my brain back—Bill takes it away from me.

And then I had to get away, frightened by catching myself in anything even resembling a trapped position.

Much as I hated men who tried to dominate me, I also came to realize that men who didn't try to rule me with an iron hand repulsed me with their weakness—a seemingly impossible dilemma, but one that proved how much I believed in the male stereotype. I resisted any concept of myself as a weak, passive woman, yet I insisted that men be strong and in control. I needed to be put under somebody's thumb, because that's where I'd been conditioned to believe I belonged. Yet I couldn't allow a man to treat me badly. My ego wouldn't stand for it.

March 16, 1969

Kyn's missing out on a good thing and he doesn't even know it. When I'm with him, he tries to take ME out of me . . . make me lose all the good things about me that attract all the people I've dug and who have dug me. He attempts to grind me down to the point where I NEED him and CRAVE him and unless I please him, I'm nobody. But I have enough faith in myself to realize that it's not MY BIG TREAT being with him —it's his privilege to be with me. He isn't hip to that. Bye-bye Kynnie . . . there will be many others.

I made up my mind to cultivate strength within myself. I wanted to establish my own sense of worth; I had seen too many crushed, emotionally exhausted females.

Yet I still needed to know that I could attract the best men. I had been conditioned to believe that a female "jock" was unattractive, so I sought as much reassurance as I could get. I had to have that phone ringing; I had to know that I was in such demand that to get any sleep I had to hide my phone in the closet and disconnect my doorbell. I used the men who came through my life at the rate of two and three a week to build that "playgirl" image, just like the playboy lifestyle so many of the guys enjoyed. Even though I cared very little for most of these phone-callers and doorbell-ringers, I liked to feel my new strength in action. I was in control because I was the one who decided whether or not I had time for them.

My drives became almost ruthless. I deliberately planned my conquests. But after a time, I grew weary of my line-'em-up-and-make-'em-wait-their-turn ego trip. Assured of my own personal and sexual power, I could "enjoy" sex without endangering my emotional life. I had enjoyed smashing the old notion of sex as sacred rite and had now turned to a philosophy of sex as sport. It felt so good to be in the driver's seat, I had to drive and drive and drive.

With one football player, the physical relationship was so good for both of us that we were both beaming from ear to ear most of the time. We often had an hour or so detour while getting dressed for his football practice and my track workout. Afterwards, that day's practice would be super. A sexually satisfied body is like a well-lubed machine: when all the parts are used and in good working order, the whole machine runs better. After a good hard afternooner with the football player, I'd have a good hard stadium-step workout and then grin. I felt like the total woman; I'd used every iota of my physical expression. Physical strength added to the whole sexual experience. How can anyone want anyone but an athlete? I asked myself.

A track meet can always be counted on for a good, healthy-minded sexual situation. As the last event, the mile relay, starts, all the athletes—except for those competing—are surveying the field. They are beginning to prepare for their own form of sex as sport. First call for the marathon. Our number one choices are checked to see if they're available. Playful open invitations are thrown out in many directions, but no commitments are made. When the mile relay is over, the serious jockeying for room keys begins. Second call for the marathon. Choice number two is putting on the pressure, but you're still holding out to see what number one has in mind. He might be tied up with the high

Washington Redskin Frank Grant and I battle it out on the racquetball court.

CREDIT: Tony Reid

jumper tonight. No, he's walking out the side exit with a hurdler, the same one he was with in Oakland last week. Oh, well, he may be free in San Diego next week. Number two is looking awfully cute tonight. Suddenly an ex-number one pops out of nowhere and coolly presses his room key into your hand. Without looking at it or acknowledging him, you slide the key into your pocket and keep rapping with the rest of the athletes who are hanging around still trying to "catch" for the night. When the last event at the meet is over for the crowd, the last event is just starting for the athletes. It is a rare athlete who stays alone in his room after a competition.

Athletes, men and women, are usually so physically

cranked up after a competition that the extra release of a good sexual workout is the only way to relax. Sprinters and jumpers are especially keyed up because they have all that adrenalin roaring through them for the meet, but their actual energy output for a meet is much less than they usually expend in a workout. We all have just experienced the pleasure and power of exertion. We have asked our bodies to do their best, and win or lose, we have all made that effort to "go beyond" ourselves. Our heads are psyched up, and our bodies are ready for more exercise. Hence, sex as sport.

Naturally, I like the best in sport and in sex, one reason I've been accused of being a body freak. I admit I am attracted primarily to championship-quality athletic bodies. ("Hey, what you got to do—run the 100 in 9.3 to get next to Huey?" a friend once joked.) But don't guys always discuss women's bodies? Don't they hope to make their women match up to a certain standard of physical attractiveness? Well, I do the same thing.

The atmosphere in the track hotels after a meet is always solid fun. I think we all feel that freedom of allowing a strong, healthy body to express itself with other strong healthy bodies. As traveling athletes we see each other in various cities around the country all season. Many people who start off as "screwin' buddies" end up as close friends; this is the healthiest kind of friendship because anxiety and jealousy is worked out from the beginning of the relationship. When we examine our sexual appetites honestly and actuate them honestly, I think we are happier, less repressed. My moments of feeling most unified with the universe, my mind and body in the most pleasant harmony, have been after my most intense and mutually satisfying sexual sessions.

The woman track athlete at these high levels of competition is tossed into social situations in which she is respected as an athlete and a person by her male counterparts. The strength required of her in athletics often will show through in her dealings with people. The spirit in the air after track encounters is fun and respectful, a direct contrast to the male–female interchange that follows pro football. I have a lot of player friends and, to some people, the time I spend with the pigskin superstars makes me a groupie. But I've found it is possible to deal with these men and their glorified superstud images when we're all doing something athletic together. I exchange athletic energies and ideas with the guys and *then* maybe get involved in a social, sexual evening.

I waited for a pro football friend outside the locker room once and vowed never to do it again. There was a spirit of male conquest in the air as the women waited like starry-eyed willing victims. I couldn't believe that so many women could let themselves be treated as hero-worshipping nobodies. Perhaps the women adopt this mentality because they have been cheering these men in the stands for three hours and have no way of snapping themselves out of that frame of mind before the guys come out of the showers. I try to fight that problem. If I appear at a motel to visit friends on teams and hopefully meet new ones, I never let my new friends get by without doing a workout of some sort with me, because I have to establish in their minds that I am an athlete, too, not just one of the sexual objects they normally herd in and out of their rooms. The guys might be tough, but they are going to know that I am athletically and mentally tough, too.

I can get to the core of these men fairly easily on an athlete-to-athlete basis. Physicalness is their way of life, so if I join them in their element, we can deal with each other honestly. On the other hand, if I were to meet these characters in a bar rather than the practice field, we would both be victims of the roles we felt we were supposed to play. The athletes' treatment as pieces of meat by their coaches often extends into their self-image, and they assume that all women see them as bodies and status-objects. Occasionally the cheerleader in me creeps out to turn me into one of their dutiful worshippers. Many times I've had to catch myself when out with one of my football friends—had to catch *both* of us—and say, "Hey it's me, remember?" We had both fallen into our roles and had to struggle out of them. Sure, it's fun to put on a show for the fans when several of us take over a bar and become the main attraction, but we have to remind ourselves after we leave that it was only a play.

My attitude toward sex and the free life frightens some men; the grapevine carries stories of superstar loves, and a man thinks "I'd better not try to deal with her." But more often because of my superstar lovers I face the opposite attitude: men make sexual advances to me because they want to be close to anything or anyone close to the superstars. A fan or a frustrated athlete feels he's some sort of star when he has the same woman that, say, a Wilt Chamberlain has had. I have to say that this is one of the more unpleasant forms of the philosophy that woman's worth is determined by the men in her life.

As an athlete I find that some men, at least at first, also have problems relating to a strong woman's body. Like one who told me, "Although half of me was very physically attracted to you, the back half of my brain was pulling away. Your body was simply outside the realm of my experience with femininity."

I find, as do many of my female athletic cohorts, that life is a lot easier if we stick with male athletes, particularly track athletes. Men who have run next to you, who have experienced the same determination and pain that you have in workouts, have a great deal of respect for a firm, well-defined body. They can appreciate the work and the effort that went into developing the strength that many other men would pull away from, be threatened by.

Most athletes I know have one very special quality: they

become addicted to a feeling of complete physical exhilaration in their own sport and seek it in all their physical experiences, whether climbing a cliff to the beach or speeding downhill on a bicycle. Athletes love physical expression, and sex is one of the best forms of it. My sexual assertiveness, like my athletic identity, is essential to my sense of self. Without it, I couldn't love life as much as I do.

I have found sex to be one of the most therapeutic, self-actualizing, and thoroughly communicative forms of expression possible. Over the years, my sexual encounters with various healthy, athletic men have been peak physical experiences, much like scuba diving in the crystal clear waters of Mexico, pouring out my entire strength in a cross country race, or catching a big wave and surfing it in to the beach.

Sex and love can be related, of course, but often they don't have to be. I enjoy experiencing the intensity of another person's sexual feelings without the ugliness of jealousy or ownership. I like to love freely, without the need to possess another human spirit. Who sets the rules that say who, when, where and why I can love? Good interpersonal relationships are too important to pass up because of some "moralist's" arbitrary rules.

Some people say to me, "Living the way you do, you'll grow old and be alone." Most people say I should protect myself against age with monogamy, a protective contract for my waning years. But I'm not interested in a security blanket, especially when it seems so emotionally expensive. Almost everyone I know who has formed "permanent" one-to-one relationships has struggled for years through a series of difficulties and finally chosen to go his or her separate way. I want to search for a better way of loving than one that obviously produces so many problems—one that doesn't seem appropriate for me. And if I find that I can be extremely happy with several people close to me, why should I trade them in and give up freedom for a traditional, exclusive love which restricts?

Prudes may call me immoral because of my sexual independence. But I trust my instincts. I need to feel autonomous. I thrive on moments when my sense of freedom is strongest, and I wither when I feel I've sacrificed myself to make another person the first priority in my life. Lord knows I love male companionship, but I also know that I need to be alone often enough to regain my sense of myself. If society respected a woman as a total independent entity instead of viewing her as a mere extension of the man closest at hand, I would probably have less of a quarrel with the one-to-one norm.

Many people who accept those social norms would, I suppose, refuse to respect my independence. The woman who demands sexual freedom is labeled promiscuous, and although men may sleep around freely, a promiscuous woman is considered sick. As Germaine Greer put it in *The Female Eunuch*,

A woman who decided to become a lover without conditions might discover that her relationships broke up relatively easily because of her degree of resistance to efforts to "tame" her.... Her promiscuity, resulting from her constant sexual desire, tenderness and interest in people, will not be differentiated from compulsive promiscuity or inability to say no, although it is fundamentally different. Her love may often be devalued by the people for whom she feels most tenderness, and her self esteem might have been under much direct attack. Such pressures cannot be utterly without effect. Even if a woman does not inhibit her behavior because of them, she will find herself reacting in some other way, being outrageous when she only meant to be spontaneous, and so forth. She may limit herself to writing defenses of promiscuity, or even books about women. (Hm.)

Greer's analysis hits home for me, for I have felt the same feelings and reactions she describes. My fight for sexual freedom has been a struggle against society and against the inhibitions and fears that society has placed in my mind. But I believe that effort has been central to my development, for every woman must control her body before she can control her mind and her life.

18

→≫ ‹‹←

A New Generation

In the fall of 1974 Wilt's WonderWomen came into existence. Formerly the La Jolla Track Club, the Wonder-Women were born when Wilt Chamberlain agreed to be a major sponsor of the club and changed its name. There are almost forty girls and women in the club, ranging in age from ten to twenty-eight. Deanne Carlsen, Patty Van Wolvelaere, Jan Svendsen, and I are the veterans of the group. Deanne, one of the few women to offer me serious competition in college, ran for Chico State College near Sacramento and is now the women's track and field coach there. She is a cute, bubbly pixie of a woman that many people have trouble believing is a serious athlete. But serious she is. Patty, a lean, energetic blonde, made her first United States team at the age of seventeen and has been one of the top two women hurdlers in the country ever since.

Much has changed since my college track years when eight or nine girls crammed into a station wagon for a drive of several hundred miles to a meet. Wilt's WonderWomen fly to many meets, one small symbol of the fact that women track athletes are at least on their way to the big time. A larger and more important symbol is the first-rate coaching our club has available. Tracy Sundlun, twenty-three, is our coach. For younger girls, Tracy provides strong leadership. For veteran athletes such as Patty and myself, he is available to offer advice; yet he also trusts our track intelligence and never overrules us if we tell him that our legs or feet are giving us trouble and need resting. A sense of humor may be Tracy's most notable personality trait, but he also knows how to maintain strict discipline. (Tracy became an assistant track coach at USC in the fall of 1975, however, a well-qualified replacement is being sought.)

Even though many of the older athletes work out at various other "home" locations most of the time, we try to get together with the team as often as possible. One warm, sunny December day, Patty, Deanne, and I grab our gear and drive to the track at the University of California, San Diego, for a workout with the team. Two of my favorite young WonderWomen run up to greet us. I swat Sheri Ball's long blond pony tail; only eleven years old and 68 pounds, she already runs the mile in 5:20.3. Lydia Laidlaw, a promising quarter-miler at 12, makes faces, pouting because Tracy is mean today.

"We have to run 660s today," she complains, but I detect anticipation in her voice. "Then we have to work on baton passes," she adds. "Tracy says you're going to help us, right?"

"Sure," I answer.

Tracy sends us on an easy mile jog to warm up, then asks each individual how she feels and what she'd like to run. I'm ready for a good hard speed workout; Patty and Deanne decide to work together on hurdle form and finish with some 220s.

Tracy puts me in charge of four younger girls to do relay passes. We each run 110 yards, pass the baton to the next girl, then rest until the baton comes back around the track. We do five 110s each, then rest and discuss any points that need correction. Then we do three more sets of five 110s each. It's a hard workout, but these girls, in their early teens, are already serious athletes. They know how to handle a baton better than I did in high school. I feel a tremendous pride watching them—so young, yet so dedicated and eager to learn.

After forty-five minutes we finish. "Okay, how does everybody feel?" I ask, and hear a lot of dramatic moans in response. But the beautiful healthy glow on their faces tells me they're all right. "Come on," I say, "let's join the girls doing 660s. If *I* can do one, *you* can do one." I want us all to have a Bud Winter-style Killer Diller finale to our workout. Then we'll go home with the natural high that comes only after all-out exertion.

Tracy stands at the 660 course finish line with his stopwatch calling out times to the first group of girls now racing toward him. Their closed eyes and open mouths tell us they are hurting, as Tracy bellows, "1:52, 1:53, 1:54. . . ." Then Tracy turns to us. "Okay ladies," he says, "I see Huey the tyrant brought you over for the kill. All right. Get ready, set, go!"

We all start quickly, then ease into a coasting stride. I'm leading, because the younger girls assume I should. I'm tired, but buoyed by the determination not to let my girls down. We cross a sandy path and begin to slip and slide, tiring even more. The path turns again between two Eucalyptus trees and we're on the home stretch. I sense the others falling back, and I grunt, "Stay with me." In an instant they're back on my tail and we all fight the last 100 yards together. Across the line, I throw my arms around the two youngest girls on the team, both are gasping, squinting in pain, obviously wondering if they're ever going to recover.

"Looking good," is all I can mutter to them because I'm wondering whether *I'm* going to recover. All of us share this moment of exhaustion and mutual pride. Real affection passes between us, and I tell myself that this is what sport is all about. Sure, each race can have only one winner, but we all can experience peak moments like this.

Wilt, as usual, dressed in a tank top, jeans, and no shoes, comes up to us, grinning his famous half-grin and nodding his head in obvious approval at our effort. "When are you all gonna work out?" he booms in our direction.

"What? Are you kidding? What do you mean?" The girls swarm over Wilt and do as much damage as they can to that giant frame. He eventually shakes them off. I love to see the girls share in the crazy teasing, the rap sessions I enjoyed so much when I worked out with the Speed City Gang. But the difference is that they are team members and don't have to listen as outsiders hoping to be included.

"You just fly in from L.A.?" I ask Wilt as I give him a swat on the rear that's right at my eye level.

"Yeah," he answers. "I knew I had to keep checking on all of your lazy asses."

Wilt's interest in women's track and his decision to sponsor our club sets an exciting precedent. We're a talented team, but there's no doubt that we've received a lot more public recognition thanks to Mr. Chamberlain. As soon as Wilt lent his name to our club, stories about us appeared in the *San Diego Union*, the *Los Angeles Times*, and *Sports Illustrated*. Wilt also gives us financial insurance. The WonderWomen team is a nonprofit organization, partially sponsored by the La Jolla Kiwanis Club, and we still need the normal gamut of fund-raising projects. But Wilt has agreed to supplement the team funds if necessary. By sponsoring the WonderWomen, Wilt puts his enormous fame to a constructive use. Possibly other sports stars, male and female, will sponsor women's athletics in the future. Yet even with Wilt on our side, our track club is continually in financial trouble. Quite simply there just isn't enough money in women's athletics

Tracy Sundlun developed the team before it had the WonderWomen name, and he has continued to press to make it one of the best track clubs in the country. He seems to have an instinctive ability to spot flaws in technique that interfere with the efficient, natural movement all athletes strive to achieve. Tracy has been developing this "coaching eye" ever since he became the unofficial manager of his high school track team at Exeter Academy in New Hampshire. At that early age Tracy also knew he would have to excel as an athlete in order to establish his own credibility as a coach. He drove himself to national-caliber rankings in squash, tennis, and waterskiing for that reason, but also so that he could share the athlete's competitive experience.

He worked under Brooks Johnson with the Sports International Track Club in Washington, D.C., and then became assistant coach at Georgetown University, on a scholarship for coaching rather than athletic services. Tracy became an Olympic coach at age twenty, when Bill Dinneen, a hammer thrower, was one of the few Puerto Ricans sent to the 1972 games. Tracy was Bill's coach at that time and was eventually selected to coach the Puerto Rican national track and field team.

When Tracy left Georgetown, he decided to form his own women's track team. His aim was to provide a women's track and field program that offered the same benefits and opportunities as a typical men's program. He came to San Luis Obispo while I was teaching at California Polytechnic State University. We jointly coached my intercollegiate women's team and his newly formed AAU track team. Both of us left San Luis Obispo after one year—I headed to Oberlin and Tracy was selected to become head coach of the La Jolla Track Club near San Diego. The club was already a major power in the women's track world, and when Tracy shifted his home base to the San Diego area,

A picnic to celebrate the birth of Wilt's WonderWomen. Front row: coach Tracy Sundlun and Patty Van Wolvelaere; above, from left: me, Cindy Gilbert, Lynne Gates, Jan Svendsen.

CREDIT: Orin Collier

so did many of the former San Luis Obispo Track Club members. Tracy was head coach of the La Jolla team for one year before I introduced him to Wilt at the California State Championships meet at UCLA in June 1974. They became friends almost immediately. Three months later, Tracy's club had become Wilt's WonderWomen and we were on our way.

Many of Tracy's concepts are new to the women's sports scene. He realized long ago that an athlete cannot be both a student and a part-time worker and still succeed at sport. For that reason, Tracy arranged scholarships for women athletes so that they could use the time they invest in athletics to gain a college education, just as men do. Patty Van Wolvelaere, who had been married and worked as a secretary for five years, could afford to come to La Jolla from Seattle because the team arranged to have her school fees and rent paid. Other athletes were offered similar arrangements. Tracy recognized that it takes money to create a top-notch athletic program, and he was willing to spend it. Long before the colleges offered financial aid to women athletes, Tracy dipped into his own trust fund to provide scholarships to women team members.

Wilt's WonderWomen also enjoy expert medical care. When we have minor aches and pains in the knees, back, or shoulders, we are sent to Dr. Leroy Perry of Pasadena, California, the team chiropractor. With his "touch for health" techniques based on acupuncture pressure points, Dr. Perry realigns our bodies and makes sure that our muscular strength is symmetrical. Dr. Perry donates his time to attend many of our track meets and take care of our precompetition needs. Dr. Charles Koscinski of La Jolla is the team podiatrist. Track athletes often have problems with their feet. I, for one, have an arthritic condition in a toe as well as occasional muscle strains in my arches. Both of these conditions have been greatly helped by the orthodics he made to fit in my shoes.

Tracy has worked hard to create an atmosphere that fosters individual excellence. Some track parents become overly involved in their daughters' careers and try to force their coaching philosophy on the team. Others push for a more recreational atmosphere. But Tracy remains firmly in control and resists any attempts to create the "cookies and punch" mentality I hated so much in college sports. Although we're all allowed to participate no matter what our level of talent or achievement, we're all expected to do our best.

Every now and then, as I watch these eager, ambitious,

and talented younger girls, I feel a twinge of regret. Where was this track club ten years ago when I needed it? But then I'm happy to know it exists now and that a new generation of women athletes is on the move. The times are indeed changing for women athletes; perhaps not as rapidly or as completely as we would like, but still the change is significant and Wilt's WonderWomen is a symbol of the new era.

There are other signs of change. A striking revision has occurred in society's standards for the female body. The natural look is in as fashion magazines feature clothes for backpacking, tennis, bowling, and other sports. And the new emphasis on fitness has helped create respect for the woman of strength and stamina.

The tone of sportswriters covering women's athletics has also changed. Most papers are killing those obnoxious features describing a woman athlete's pretty legs and long blond hair and noting that she really doesn't look like an athlete. Reflecting the new respect for women's sport, *Sports Illustrated* recently covered the women's national intercollegiate basketball championships as a serious journalistic event. Spectacular play, not spectacular looks, was the angle of the story, and the reader was presented with a game, not a girlie show. Now potential women athletes can find role models in the sports pages just as boys do. Young girls can flip through the pages of *WomenSport*, the magazine published by Billie Jean and Larry King, and find their own real-life heroines. More sports coverage like this will be an important factor in helping women athletes create audiences.

The mass media also are providing much more coverage of women's events. I noticed the difference in 1975 when I coached at Mira Costa College in Oceanside, California, and had no difficulty in convincing the local paper to print the results of our volleyball games. Two years earlier in San Luis Obispo, I found it next to impossible to get press coverage of my track news. In my opinion, the *Los Angeles*

Times has led the way in providing good coverage for women athletes; a woman's sporting event appears on the front page of the sports section regularly. Other papers are beginning to provide steady coverage, especially of local sports heroines and locally important sports. Overall coverage of women's sports still isn't as good as it should be, but at least newspapers recognize the need to improve and are making changes.

Television also is doing a better job of covering women's sports, although the coverage still reinforces some of the feminine stereotypes. Francie Larieu, world-record holder in the mile, is charming in an interview, but the audience doesn't often see how she sweats and drives herself to track triumphs. The moments of strength and courage are usually left to the male athletes the viewer will see.

Donna DeVerona, sportscaster for ABC, represents a major breakthrough as one of the first women to hit big-time sports media. Donna is a good journalist, but it's no accident that she's also a beauty. No one tells Curt Gowdy he can't broadcast a football game because he doesn't look like everybody's dream man, but a woman sportscaster apparently still has to be attractive. ABC also took an important step forward when it devoted two full hours of prime time to the women's SuperStars competition. Top women professional athletes were exposed to the sporting public for the first time in a sports medley. As these and other women athletes become familiar to the public, the audience for women's events can be expected to grow.

Young girls today are increasingly able to join competitive teams in a variety of sports as high schools, for the first time, offer serious athletics to young women. The California Interscholastic Federation began to hold both boys' and girls' events at its state championships track meet in 1973, and schools across the country are opening intra- and intermural competition to girls. When girls can't find team sports in school they look elsewhere—witness the controversy that forced the Little Leagues to admit girls.

College athletic programs also are improving, in part because of pressure from federal legislation. Title IX of the Education Amendments of 1972 forbids sex-discriminatory programs in educational institutions that receive federal funds. Although many women have been disappointed by Title IX's serious deficiencies (for example, schools are not required to spend equal aggregate amounts for programs for men and women) there can be no doubt that the law has forced educational institutions to reevaluate their programs, and women have benefited.

According to Joyce Malone, women's athletic director at San Jose State, my own alma mater has made significant improvements in its women's sports programs. When I arrived at SJS in 1965, the total budget for women's sports was $4,000. Today, the women have a budget of $22,700 for a program of six intercollegiate sports. Not that women are even close to equality at SJS. For example, some $300,000 is spent on men's football alone, and women have a budget of $3,600 for basketball compared with $62,000 for men's.

But at least women students now do have a full-time women's athletic director to administer their program. A half-time trainer and a fully equipped training room, complete with whirlpools, hydrocolaters, and ice machines, are also available. Each women's team now has uniforms and warm-up suits in SJS's colors of blue and gold, a marked improvement over my college days. When SJS women's teams travel, they now fly to their destination if necessary, and in 1975–1976, SJS will issue grants-in-aid to women athletes for the first time.

Other colleges have also beefed up their women's sports programs. According to the *Los Angeles Times*, Barbara Hedges, the director of women's sports at the University of Southern California (USC), now spends a total of $100,000 annually for her program compared to $11,000 a year ago. Long Beach State College increased its budget for women's sports to $41,000 from $21,000 in the past year. Again, women are a long way from financial equality; USC spends $2.5 million for men's sports and Long Beach invests $145,000 in men's activities not counting football and basketball, which run on separate budgets.

Women should be proud of the gains they are making in sports programs, but they should not be content with token improvements. Men's programs continue to generate more alumni support and larger audiences, one reason colleges use to justify larger budgets for men. But until women are adequately funded, they will not be able to develop the kinds of programs and the quality of competition that attracts attention and outside support. Women are just beginning to break the vicious circle of poverty in women's sports, and this trend must continue.

Another recent change is the establishment of the Association for Intercollegiate Athletics for Women (AIAW), organized in 1972 to serve as the women's equivalent of the men's National Collegiate Athletic Association (NCAA). Most colleges in the country now belong to AIAW, which governs intercollegiate competition in seven sports: golf, badminton, gymnastics, track and field, volleyball, swimming and diving, and basketball.

The organization already has come a long way. Initially it forbade athletic scholarships for women, largely in reaction to the abuses that have gone on so long in funding male athletes. This ruling left schools such as Tennessee State, which had long given women track scholarships, ineligible to compete for intercollegiate national titles. But in 1974, women athletes put on the pressure. They were tired of all the bucks passing them by, and wanted their crack at "equal opportunity exploitation." So the AIAW changed its policy, and now there are more than sixty colleges offering athletic scholarships. Recruiting, however, is usually sluggish; the burden is still on the women to make the initial contact.

Patty Van Wolvelaere is now attending USC on a full tuition and fees athletic scholarship. Although Patty is a two-time Olympian, and is nationally ranked higher than 99 percent of all track men on scholarship, she doesn't receive twice-monthly stipends as they do. Instead she must scramble for part-time work to pay the rent. America's best female hurdler, although receiving one of the best scholarship offers for women in the country still isn't as well taken care of as a mediocre male athlete. Imagine the treatment of promising, but as yet unproven, women athletes.

Meanwhile, the Amateur Athletic Union's sports programs for women have also made significant gains. Nationwide statistics on participation are not kept—each of AAU's fifty-eight districts across the country registers its own athletes. However, Dan Ferris, AAU secretary emeritus, offers an educated guess that the number of women involved in AAU track has jumped from a few thousand ten years ago to some 50,000 actively competing today. "We now have so many fine women athletes that we are able to take a full crew to Europe with us each summer," Ferris added. "Our talent has increased and so have foreign requests to have our women compete in meets abroad."

AAU facilities for women's events today are a far cry from the ones I knew as an aspiring athlete ten years ago. Big state and national championships normally are held on the new synthetic tracks at college campuses such as UCLA or UC, Irvine. Equipment such as wind gauges and timers as well as more knowledgeable officials are now available.

Yet inequities still exist. Many indoor AAU meets held during the winter offer numerous events for men but provide only a few token races for women. On the west coast, indoor meets are the most pleasant time of the entire track season, because they are viewed as the "fun, get ready" part of the season. They involve much less pressure than the major outdoor track competitions. Success or failure in most indoor meets has little effect on an athlete's national ranking, yet the athlete has a chance to run in front of large audiences and build a reputation. Women still don't stand an equal chance.

Unfair treatment in meets has angered many women athletes for years, and in 1974 Jan Svendsen, Patty Van Wolvelaere, and I tried to do something about it. The Sunkist Indoor Track Meet in Los Angeles offered only four women's events compared to thirty-two events for men and boys. Since many of the nation's best women long jumpers, high jumpers, and sprinters live in the Los Angeles area, the meet organizers had no excuse for limiting women's competition. They would not even have to pay expensive airfares and hotel bills to gather an impressive collection of women athletes. My friends and I decided to stage a protest and printed flyers listing the national- and Olympic-caliber women athletes who live in California and could have come to the meet. We also posted large petitions demanding more women's events in future Sunkist meets. We gathered more than three hundred signatures supporting our position, but not everyone was enthusiastic about the prospect of more women's events.

"I can't stand to watch women do anything on the track," said one memorable MCP. "Four events is too many already," said another. As I took these insults, I realized that male chauvinism is one of the few prejudices that's still socially acceptable. If we had been blacks taking a stand on a racial issue, our opponents probably would have kept their thoughts to themselves. Undaunted, we collected our supporting signatures and presented the petition to Al Franken, the meet manager. Our effort paid off in 1975, when the Sunkist meet scheduled eight women's events.

The indoor season has long been lucrative for men track athletes, and at last women are beginning to get their share of the booty. I took home my first real prize—a digital clock —after the San Diego Indoor Games last year. I may owe my prize in part to Patty Van Wolvelaere. The year before in the *San Francisco Examiner* meet, she received a cheap trophy (when the men were taking home TV's and tape recorders) and promptly threw it into the stands to indicate her displeasure. This year, she took home an AM-FM clock radio, the same prize awarded to Tommie Lee White, winner of the men's hurdles.

Women today are beginning to be taken as serious track athletes by a larger proportion of the population. Both Patty and I have been pleasantly surprised to have young male track athletes gather around to watch us practice starts or do baton-passing drills. Now men seem willing to admit that they can learn from a woman athlete. And the insulting restrictions on women's athletic efforts are slowly being eliminated. In 1972 women ran the Olympic metric mile for the first time, and more and more women are running longer distances, proving that the female body is capable of withstanding the strain. Indeed, hundreds of women are attempting the ultimate distance race, the marathon. No matter where you are now, be it Central Park or the UCLA practice fields, you can see more women running than ever before.

The AAU has even organized a master's division to allow women over twenty-five to continue to participate in track by competing in their own age group. In 1974 I attended my first "old ladies' Olympics" as I called them, at the University of California at Irvine. Fewer than ten women participated, but I expect the number will soar as the years go by. The meet left me with a tremendous sense of achievement as Cherri Sherrard, former Olympic hurdler, and I competed for our own "Grandma Track" title. Cherri won the 100 meters, but I had a faster time in the 200 meters the next day. We both set national records for our age groups and walked off with gold medals—not bad for two oldsters.

Professional track finally became a reality in 1973, when the International Track Association signed more than fifty

Cherri Sherrard and me setting our starting blocks for the master's division 100-yard dash in 1974 at the University of California at Irvine.

CREDIT: Patty Van Wolvelaere

men and four women. Women's participation is barely noteworthy—women compete in one 60-yard dash compared to more than a dozen events for men. Still, women receive the same prize money, and that's a start. Meet organizers have experimented with coed events and found audiences receptive.

All the new excitement surrounding women's track, indeed all women's sport, promises healthier, more alive, more confident women in the future. The benefit of sport, the sound body that is the seat of a sound mind, will now accrue to women who no longer need feel defensive about their love of vigorous activity. Even old ladies like myself are exhilarated by the change.

The new excitement in women's track at the AAU National last year prompted an entry in my diary:

June 27, 1974

What a complete turnabout . . . the men are coming to watch US. Complete people here getting ready to do their own thing. LOVE IT! I'm anchoring the 440 relay and running a 110 leg on the 880 medley relay. The carriage, the confidence of all these women athletes is beautiful . . . such a good team feeling too. Didn't realize what a good thing I missed all these years. Just missed my era I guess. Should be young now and could do anything!

19

>>> <<<

An Athlete, A Woman

"What is this out here—a circus?" Donald Riggs yelled. "All right. Anyone not on the track team, out! From now on this track will be off limits to everyone except the track team from 2 to 5 P.M."

Riggs, assistant coach of track and field at San Jose State, had a point. Dogs ran loose, bike riders wandered across the track at will, and joggers plodded along on inside lanes, interfering with sprinters and distance runners who were trying to get 220 and 330 interval times. Riggs had just come from Oregon State (he was hired by Ernie Bullard, Bud Winter's successor), and the lax atmosphere at SJS made him furious.

But how could he eliminate everyone not on the track team? George Carty, Lee Evans, Vic Dias, and I were alumni, so it was still our track. I was certain he wasn't about to throw us out. I was partly right: he wasn't about to throw *them* out.

"I'm closing the track to everyone but the track team," Riggs said to Lee, who was taking starts in the lane next to me. "But I want you to know that you're welcome. Anytime you want to join us, feel free, but no one else is going to be allowed to practice here." Riggs was speaking loudly to Lee. Obviously, he wanted me to hear. The nerve, I thought, to try to make me feel unwanted on my track. I've left as much sweat out there as anyone else, and I was determined not to let him discriminate against me.

Riggs repeated his routine with Vic. I ignored the less than subtle hints. I set myself in the blocks with Lee and took a gun start. I reacted first but Lee had me by about 3 yards by the time we were out 20 yards or so. We walked back to the starting line. Now Riggs approached me and told me directly to leave. He was cool and collected, but so was I. I calmly explained that I had trained on the track for six years, and that I belonged.

"But we're closing the track to anyone not on the team," he said.

"But not to the alumni, I notice, except for me," I said.

Then, for an instant, Riggs went berserk. He stuttered, cursed, turned red and finally exploded, "God damn it, you've gotta get off my track!"

After cooling down, he said, "Wait a minute. Lee and George can help us recruit. What can you do for us?"

"Has it occurred to you that maybe I was here before Lee and George and that I helped recruit *them,*" I said. "I think what this basically boils down to is that you don't want women on your track."

"Oh, hell," Riggs shouted. "I've got a damned women's libber on my hands on top of all my other problems."

At this point, Lee, lying on the track, started slapping the tartan in fits of laughter. Riggs stomped around a little more then regained his composure.

"Isn't there any chance that you could practice another time?" he asked.

I ran my timetable down to him and proved that the only reasonable time for me to come to the track was at about 3 each afternoon.

"Okay," he said, "but don't you get in the way of my athletes like all the rest of these idiot joggers."

"I'm well aware of the rules of the track," I answered icily. "I won't be in anybody's way."

Even though I no longer felt like working out, I had to stay there and make my presence felt so that Riggs would know that I had triumphed in our confrontation. I wanted to be able to come back whenever I wanted without having to endure another public battle. I ran some 110s in as close to perfect form as I could; then without a word I marched off the track.

I had changed a lot to make that recent victory over Riggs possible. Earlier I would not have dared to confront him. Men were right; they were the ones who made the decisions. Women might have lives of their own, but only if their independence didn't interfere with their relationships with men. A woman who didn't receive male approval was a failure, or so it seemed to me. I wanted to be respected as a serious, dedicated athlete during practice, but I also needed to know that I was attractive to men. I was the entertainer, diverting my energies to amuse all the men around me. I had a million acts to prove that no matter how strong I appeared, I was just a silly little girl around my men. Even my sexual assertiveness added up to the same search for approval—I was proud to be the most physical female my man had ever experienced. Most of the men in my life wanted a man-focused woman. If I let the strong part of me show, they backed off until my "helpless" personality resurfaced. I knew how to keep the already swollen egos of my male friends at the bursting point. They liked me that way, and that's the way I stayed.

I had developed two sets of body language, two distinct manners. My friends saw me as strong-minded, full of ideas, proud of my independence. My lovers saw me as wide-eyed, believing anything they said, carrying myself as if I didn't have a muscle in my body. I had also developed two sets of relationships: Super Buddy was the man I talked with and trusted; Super Love was my romantic, physical ideal. I could spend all the time in the world with my Buddies, but I had to exchange sexual energies, then run from my Loves. I refused to trust any one man with access to both my mind and my body. I was bordering on schizophrenia.

One day as I drove from San Francisco to San Diego with my usual stops in San Jose, San Luis Obispo, Santa Barbara, and Los Angeles, to see my usual men, I realized that I must seem like a cartoon character. I zoomed in and out of lives like the roadrunner. I was never going to allow anyone to become an indispensable part of my life so I kept on the move, figuring no one could harm me. I started rethinking my relationships with these men. I knew that I cared about them, that they were my close friends, and friends shouldn't have to play games to avoid trusting each other. "What am I doing?" I asked myself.

I had been famous for one-nighters. Now I became more selective. I let my already formed male friendships evolve into more complex relationships with my favorite men.

I began making progress toward real positive friendships with the various men in my life with whom I had always spent time but had never been able to give much of myself to before. The more I changed the more I realized that the men in my life were different now, too. The women's movement had made many of my men aware for the first time of their male chauvinist attitudes. My black friends, who were all too well aware of the struggle they face in white society, tried especially hard to understand what it means to be female in a male-dominated culture. One night after a track meet, several friends and I passed up the usual post track meet romp to go to my house and talk. We sat up until five in the morning wrestling with new insights we had discovered in our dealings with people. My male friends told me that they knew the traditional male–female roles are stifling to women. But at the same time, they protested, the male is often drained because he has to supply all the initiative and direction for the pair. Too often, they complained, women toss the responsibility for their own lives onto their men, an abdication that hurts us all. We agreed that male–female relationships must change to relieve men of this overwhelming burden and to free women from lives of emotional dependence and self-sacrifice.

Fewer of my close male friends are living double lives now. I had been leading the free, roving life of the male, but without the arrogant knowledge that I, like many male friends, would have someone at home waiting for me. Few men would put up with a woman running the streets while they stayed home. But why should I share the freedom that I had to fight so hard for with men who were perpetuating the oppressed female relationships at home? Why should I share my hard-earned freedom with men who weren't strong enough to reach my point of self-reliance?

Day-to-day practice of these new-found insights has been difficult. But now at least I realize that we're on the right path. I want male companionship still, but I know that I can be a total person without it. And when acquaintances tell me that someday I'll settle down and find the right *man*, I tell them that I've already found and am still finding the right *men*.

I think that for the first time I've managed to combine the "Super Buddies" and the "Super Loves." I no longer interact with men purely on a physical basis as I did for so long. Now I enjoy discovering a man's totality, no longer afraid to share that much of myself in return. I have ex-

perienced phases of security in these new-found relationships and independence and now I feel more comfortable
with myself than ever before. Dealing with several men on
this basis means exchanging valuable human moments
when we are together, and not having a crushing sense of
loss when we part. As a lawyer friend of mine says, "If I
don't see you later, I'll see you later." With good friends,
later always comes.

And today good friends are not necessarily men. As a
result of my athletic and identity struggles, I had learned
to dislike other women, and for a long time I thought I had
nothing in common with members of my own sex. Now I
am finding a new breed of female, women who rebelled just
as much as I did. They too had felt confined in that rigid
female stereotype and wanted out. They too had established themselves in their minds and in their relationships
as strong, complete human beings who happened to be
women.

Edna Long, the dance instructor at Federal City, is an
example. With her own money, initiative, and drive, she
developed a performing company of five talented dancers
called "Chocolate City." Today, Edna and I talk about
much more than the men in our lives when we're together.
Now we share contacts and professional knowledge. We
talk about the business world, how it operates and what it
takes to succeed. I've spent hours in the past listening silent
and wide-eyed while my men friends talked "business."
Now I'm interested in that outside world myself. My
women friends have helped me learn how to go out into the
world and get a piece of it for myself.

Peg Summers, a close friend in New York, amazes and
inspires me with her gutsiness. When she was thirty, her
husband died of diabetes. Within four short years she has
managed to pull her life back together, has studied a year
in Ireland (she just packed up her three kids and left, determined she could make it), and has recently bought a loft in

Greenwich Village. All these decisions to create change were hard for her, sure, but she is one strong woman at this point. She knows that she can make decisions on her own that not only affect herself but the lives of her children.

Her children remind me that sexual stereotypes *can* be dissolved with insightful guidance. The girl and two boys discover the world with the same eagerness for exploration. Already, at ages twelve, nine, and six, they are independent little people who are innovative and creative. Their mother had always been a rebel of sorts—dressing, saying, and doing what she felt like—and they are already on their way to being what they themselves can and want to be, not what outside pressures would force them to be.

My sister Margie, after six years of marriage, decided to pack her 1955 Ford Fairlane and drive from San Jose to Detroit to begin working on her Ph.D. at the age of thirty. This move is all the more remarkable when you consider that she had seldom been out of San Jose and had a husband whom she loved, yet with whom she knew she couldn't reach her full individual potential. He wouldn't leave his postman's job in San Jose, so Margie found the nerve to go ahead with her plans alone. She had to buck protests from our folks and other relatives for several months before the move. "You can't just desert your husband; your place is by his side." These people seemed more concerned with her husband's comfort than with Margie's intellectual and personal growth. Yet most of her female friends wished her luck saying, "I could never do it; I admire your guts." Now she has one year's study left in her Ph.D. program in speech and communication and has become a published researcher.

Patty Van Wolvelaere and I met in January 1974 and clicked instantly. We both had felt like freaks all our lives. Now I know that there's another woman in the world who resembles me in physical, social, and psychological needs and who satisfies those needs much the same way I do.

Patty has helped me understand that activities I've considered male are equally female—if women treat them seriously. When I was at San Jose State, I never felt that my workouts with women were as significant as the time I spent with the men's track team. Now Patty and I work out on various tracks in California and I feel the confidence in myself as a legitimate athlete that I previously received only in male company. Patty and I make a great duo in social situations, too. Normally, the men talk and the women sit around and grin approval. But Patty and I generate so much electricity together that the men take us on our terms. Patty and I have had some outrageous escapades together, but recently we've toned down our act. We no longer feel we have to prove anything.

I see now that for too long I allowed myself to be overwhelmed by images. My men friends were celebrated in the newspapers; the Speed City Gang were folk heroes in San Jose, and my Eagle, 49er and Redskin buddies were legends in their home towns. I felt I could become part of the news by knowing names in the news. I lurked in the shadows behind every sports story. I allowed *Sports Illustrated*, the *Los Angeles Times*, and the *Washington Post* to build these men into figures I worshipped instead of men I really knew. Recently, as I've fought images of femininity that have so undermined my independence, I have also understood the need to break apart the images that surround my friends.

Wilt Chamberlain, for example, has always been the star of stars. Well-known men become hero worshippers when tossed unexpectedly into his presence. We joked and jabbed at each other over the years and I thought we had developed our own brand of friendship. Now I realize that for a long time I didn't relate to him as a man with normal needs and wants. I had been fooled by the hard exterior Wilt developed to protect himself against a rude, intruding public.

"Don't you think sometimes that since your image is so powerful in people's minds you might fall victim to it and begin to live that image for them?" I once asked him. He admitted the possibility did exist.

All the false images that destroy an individual's ability to be his or her most human, most creative self must be shattered. For some, the image is custom-tailored; a sports star is described in a certain way in the papers and then becomes the person he's read about. Others are constricted by general images. For women it is the traditional feminine stereotype: anything strong, powerful, and positive is viewed as masculine, whereas anything weak, powerless, and passive is seen as feminine. If strength, confidence, and an assured manner are masculine, then many women athletes have developed masculine traits. But I prefer to see the new woman another way: a woman who is strong is not masculine; she is a *strong woman.*

Each of us also has a central part of our personality that should not be denied. The peak moments of my life have involved physical exertion, and during periods when I have abandoned or been forced to abandon athletics, I have not been myself. My body and mind both thrive on the moments of physical challenge that hard workouts bring. My body aches and my mind screams when I'm unable to work out. My mood crumbles, and the optimist in me sees a dreary world. I've learned that physical expression means too much to me ever to consider giving it up again. I know that the times I feel old, afraid that my body is failing me, are the times that I'm not actively involved in physical activity. When I'm in shape, I feel as if age can't touch me. I feel as if I'm not getting older; I'm just getting better.

At age twenty-seven I began to run cross-country and conditioned myself into the best shape of my life. I weighed ten pouunds less than I had in college and felt stronger than ever. As a sprinter I had never thought seriously about distance running, but now I lived on the beach and it seemed natural to run four to six miles every day. So when Tracy Sundlun announced that Wilt's WonderWomen would again sponsor its annual cross-country meet, I was excited. My sprinter's conditioning had never before permitted me to run cross-country distance, a mile and three quarters in competition. This year, I took the challenge.

I wake up the morning of the race free of anxiety, but full of anticipation. "It doesn't matter how well I do," I reassure myself. "People won't expect as much of me in this race because I'm known as a sprinter." I arrive at the meet feeling as if I have everything to gain and nothing to lose. Not even Wilt's good-natured teasing can daunt me. But as I jog part of the course with a few other sprinters, I sense what is in store for me and begin to feel my first butterflies.

I'm worried. I shouldn't have had any breakfast. That juice and piece of toast feel like lead. All I can do is hope that by race time, an hour away, the heaviness will be gone. I'm pleased to see that I can easily jog over a mile for my warm-up without losing strength.

The hour passes quickly and soon all the young distance runners are lining up for the start. Wilt is the starter and he's been having trouble with the gun. Twice already he's had to yell "Go!" because the gun didn't fire. I hope that doesn't happen in my race, because I know I'll start laughing. The mood of the runners is relaxed, jovial—a sharp contrast to the atmosphere at the start of a sprint. Everyone knows that the first moments of the race aren't that important. The test will come much later.

As the gun fires, my sprinter's instinct leads me to jump ahead of the pack. Then I realize what I've done and settle in to the group's pace. I see the four best distance runners from our team take the lead and I decide to let them go. I'm a sprinter and I don't want to burn myself out to stay with them now and have to crawl in embarrassed at the end. The front pack moves about 10 yards ahead of me and two other sprinters who make up the second pack. Our competitive instinct makes us want to move ahead but we don't know what we're up against yet and hesitate to assert ourselves.

After a long straightaway, the path turns, crosses the roadway, and enters a grove of eucalyptus trees. We wind down a sandy pathway. I can tell which girls have run the course before; they are able to choose the most solid ground. I follow their lead. At the bottom of the path we turn and begin to climb a hill. The sprinter to my right is already beginning to tire. "Come on Linda, stay up," I say to encourage her. She stays with me for another 400 yards, but then she eases up, leaving me to go after the front pack, still 10 to 15 yards ahead.

We approach a hill. My mind clicks back to all the stadium slope workouts I did with Billy Gaines in San Jose, and I decide to *run* that hill. Now the real struggle of the race begins. I drive past two of the younger girls from another team with little effort. I try to pass a small girl in pigtails in front of me, but she keeps moving into my path every time I try to go by. Finally, I reach down and hold her to my left as I pass her on the right. She tries to challenge my move, but after 20 or 30 yards she lets me go.

I keep on driving, gradually closing in on the leaders. Near the top of the hill, I catch up with two more girls and cruise by them on the run down the other side. I am now in third place, but I have paid a price. A sensation of incredible heat in my head and nausea warns me of pain to come.

I have no idea how far I've run, but I hope I'm at least halfway home. We all keep the same pace, maintaining our relative positions for another quarter mile or so, then turn onto another path. Bill Dinneen, Tracy's assistant coach, stands at the turn holding a marker.

"Less than a mile, Huey," he says to encourage me.

"Hell," I mutter as I realize that I have further to go than I thought. Now I have visions of limping through the rest of the race. I could always claim that a shoelace broke, that I have a stitch in my side, a cramp in my calf. After all, I am a sprinter; no one can expect much of me in a distance race.

But only 1 percent of me wants to find excuses for defeat. The other 99 percent is saying no, I'm going to give it everything I have. I'm going to face this pain head on. I'm going to test myself deeper than I've ever tried to before. I want to see what I can do when I hold nothing back.

I swing my arms harder, forcing longer, more powerful strokes that lengthen and strengthen my stride. I am totally drained. All the muscle fuel I had is burned up, and I'm running on empty. I'm not afraid of the pain, the sense of impending exhaustion; I've known that feeling before and I'm purposefully pushing into it now.

I round the last turn and start running down a slope. My vision blurs. Unable to focus my eyes, I'm afraid I might trip on a rough spot on the path. I decide to ignore that worry and let instinct guide me down the path.

On flat ground again, I race those 300 yards to the finish. I can practically smell the tape, and a jolt of adrenalin surges through my body. The sprinter in me resurfaces and I run those last yards in high-knee, full driving form. I love every minute of this pain, which is flooding through my body, because I can control it. It doesn't control me. The crowd watching applauds as I come in third after our two best distance runners, but I don't really hear them. I am totally absorbed in this test of myself.

A final wave of pain hits as I relax the defenses that have kept my body's protests at bay. I feel an enormous pride at having conquered this new challenge. I am happy with myself—athlete, woman, individual. I would love to be able to go on running forever.

Wilt watches as I pass the finish line, exhausted, but much happier than I look.

CREDIT: Micki McGee/ISSS

DATE			